AIMLESS LIFE, AWESOME GOD

ROBERT FROHLICH

Copyright © 2016 by Robert Frohlich

Aimless Life, Awesome God
by Robert Frohlich

Printed in the United States of America.

Edited by Elizabeth Armbrecht

Back cover photo: Lee VanKoningsveld

Website: RobertFrohlichAuthor.com

ISBN 9781498477970

All rights reserved solely by the author. The author guarantees all contents are original and do not infringe upon the legal rights of any other person or work. No part of this book may be reproduced in any form without the permission of the author. The views expressed in this book are not necessarily those of the publisher.

The prayer found on page 154 is reprinted from *A Guide to Prayer for All God's People* by Rueben P. Job and Norman Shawchuck. Copyright © 1990. Used by permission of Upper Room Books. books.upperroom.org.

Unless otherwise indicated, Scripture quotations taken from:

The English Standard Version (ESV). Copyright © 2001 by Crossway, a publishing ministry of Good News Publishers. Used by permission. All rights reserved.

The King James Version (KJV) – *public domain.*

www.xulonpress.com

TABLE OF CONTENTS

Acknowledgements. .ix

Chapter 1—France, March 30, 1962 11
Chapter 2—What's My Name? 14
Chapter 3—Daddy 17
Chapter 4—A Family 22
Chapter 5—A Good Scout. 35
Chapter 6—Saved 39
Chapter 7—The Best and Worst of Times. . 46
Chapter 8—Escape From New York 62
Chapter 9—Bigger Wheels 71
Chapter 10—A New Direction. 78
Chapter 11—Another Country 90
Chapter 12—The Past Catches Up 98
Chapter 13—My Plan, God's Plan. 102
Chapter 14—A New Life 113
Chapter 15—Moving Up. 123
Chapter 16—Friends and Family 131
Chapter 17—Not Quite Billy Graham 141
Chapter 18—An Ordinary Witness 148
Chapter 19—To Boldly Go 156
Chapter 20—Whatever happened to. 161

Dedicated to the memory of

Ella and Don Plitt
Kay and Charlie Zittel

Wonderful people who helped me
in my time of greatest need

Acknowledgements

This book would not have been written except for the inspiration and help of my friend and former colleague, Barbara Bras. When she published her first book, *Wrapped in God's Grace: A Life Rediscovered*, I bought it and read it in one sitting; it was that good. It made me realize that it was high time I wrote my story: how God intervened in my life, saved my life, and changed my life to make me the man He wanted me to be. Barbara has been a mentor and accountability partner throughout this whole process.

Thanks also to Bob Holzinger and Bob Warner, fellow Elders from the First Reformed Church in Racine, Wisconsin, for acting as accountability partners and who prayed me through to the finish.

I'm especially grateful for the editing skills of Elizabeth Armbrecht, who gently applied discipline and brought out the best in what I intended to write.

To my patient wife, Marleen, who put up with me being locked away in my office while I sweated this out, thanks. And to our daughters, Robin Armbrecht and Starr Frohlich, thanks for your prayers.

Finally, and most importantly, thanks be to God, for giving me a life worth writing about.

> "I shall not die, but I shall live,
> and recount the deeds of the Lord."
> Psalm 118:17 ESV

Chapter 1

FRANCE, MARCH 30, 1962

I came to lying on my back in the middle of the road, looking up at the gray sky. It was still drizzling, and the pavement was wet; rivulets of water trickled off the blacktop toward the shoulder of the road. There was no pain. "Oh God, can I move? Am I paralyzed? Is anything broken?" Gingerly, I wiggled my fingers and toes, moved my arms and legs a little, then slowly I sat up. "Thank you, God." Now, where were the guys who were riding with me in the Jeep, and were they okay?

In fall 1961, when our outfit moved into the Sidi Brahim Caserne, a former French prison camp turned U.S. Army base, my friend Tom and I took a walk around town.

He'd been in France about six months longer than I had and was an expert on all things French. As we walked by the highway department yard, Tom pointed out the white-painted road markers stacked along a wall. "If you ever hit one of those, don't worry," he said. "They're hollow."

I had been taking two men from our outfit back to base in the late afternoon on a rural road in France, somewhere between Verdun and Etain. I liked to take shortcuts, get off the main roads, and find different ways to get from point A to point B. I argued with my company commander that it would be useful to know my way around in case of war. It had been raining. The last things I remembered were the stupid vacuum windshield wipers slowing down, the crappy tactical tires losing grip, a sharp curve to the left in the road ahead, and a white road marker dead-on in front of me.

As I surveyed the accident scene, it was apparent that the Jeep had gone straight off the road, hit and dislodged the white road marker, sideswiped a large tree, and rolled over back onto the pavement where it came to rest on its left side, the driver's side. I also noted that my body had been laying an arm's length from the bottom of the Jeep, between the Jeep and the tree. The Jeep had missed landing on me by about three feet. How was it possible that I had been

France, March 30, 1962

ejected from the Jeep but not squashed like a bug when it landed on its side?

I walked around to the top side of the Jeep and found my two riders standing dazed and looking for me. I posted one guy farther around the curve to warn any oncoming drivers. The other guy walked with me back to the main highway where I hoped we could flag down an army vehicle to go for help. A truck stopped, and we explained the situation. The driver said he'd send help and asked if we needed an ambulance. I said no, but my buddy took one look at the blood flowing from the back of my head and said, "Yes, we need one."

Help arrived, and we were all taken back to the hospital at Verdun, where we were treated for minor injuries. The MP's (military police) questioned me thoroughly and ordered a blood test to check for alcohol. It came out clean since I didn't drink back then. We got a ride back to our barracks in Etain, arriving about midnight. I promptly went to my buddy Tom's bunk and shook him awake. When he opened his eyes I said, "They're not hollow."

That was not the only time God saved my life.

"For my father and my mother have forsaken me, but the Lord will take me in."
Psalm 27:10 ESV

Chapter 2

WHAT'S MY NAME?

I was born Robert William Kaufman Jr. in Queens, New York in January 1943 and was baptized at St. John's Lutheran Church in February 1943. Now right there you can see that things don't always wind up where they start out. My name on the front cover of this book is different from the one above, and I'm not the one who changed it. The "aimless" aspect of this story starts right away; I was born with one name, grew up with another, and I had nothing to do with it. And that name change would be the first act of God that saved my life in the ultimate sense.

My grandparents, Wilhelm and Elsbeth Buethner, came to the United States from

Germany with their only child, Ursula, in the late 1920s. On Ellis Island, their name was changed to Burtner. They eventually settled in College Point, New York, where Wilhelm (now William) and Elsbeth learned to speak English. William worked as a common laborer until his command of the language was sufficient to work as a skilled tool and die maker, which was the trade he had learned in Berlin, Germany.

Although the Burtners were not religious, Ursula was confirmed at the age of thirteen in St. John's Lutheran Church. She grew up wanting to be a nurse, but her parents thought that would be unseemly. Later, with the war on, she went to work at Edo Aircraft in College Point, where William was the shop supervisor. There she met Robert Kaufman, and they were married in February 1942. Ursula was excited about her new life, dreaming of independence from her parents and a happy married life with Bob. Bob joined the Navy on August 9, 1943, following in his father's footsteps as a sailor. Ursula's dream quickly died. Off to war went Bob, and Mom was stuck, living with her parents, full of resentment. I was just eight months old, so I never knew him. The first time God saved my life came shortly thereafter.

We lived in a home on a double lot on 122nd street. I don't remember much else about that house. In the side yard Grandma Burtner grew herbs that she used for cooking, and there was a grape arbor. We lived together there: the Burtners, great-grandpa Gustav Schultz, Mom, and me. There is a picture, taken next to the house, of Mom, my father in his Navy uniform, and me. That photo was torn in two and taped back together. I think Mom did that.

Access to the basement in this house was through a trap door leading to a steep stairway that ended near the big coal furnace. I was a toddler then, just learning to get around in my walker. I raced down the hallway with nary an adult in sight toward the wide open trap door. And down I went. Now, of course, I don't remember this event. It was related to me many years later by my mother. I somehow survived without any cuts or broken bones and only a slight indentation in my forehead to show for my tumble.

Where I live today, we have a neighbor, Danny, who, when he was seventeen, dove into the water and broke his neck. He is a quadriplegic nearing the age of fifty. When I see Danny outside in his motorized wheelchair and wave to him across the lawn, I can't help but think how my tumble back then might have had a much worse result.

"...and you shall be called by a new name
that the mouth of the Lord will give."
Isaiah 62:2b ESV

Chapter 3

DADDY

Mom divorced my father Bob in 1945, he still in the Navy, and she still frustrated with life at home raising a child. And it only got worse. Mom resented having to live with her parents who were always quick to judge her. She worked as a hairdresser and hated it. The Burtners were very proper folks, and this daughter's life did not fit the image they tried to maintain. What would people think? That's a phrase I heard over and over again as I grew up.

I loved my mother. She was beautiful, with dark brown hair and deep brown eyes. In photos, she always looked lovely, but rarely was there a smile on her face. But Mom did have a great sense of humor, and as I grew up, we used to talk and laugh and play long games of Canasta, a card game. Mom would tell me about her dreams and yearnings as a young girl. She loved the 1940s, the dancing, the music. I liked it when she played her Glenn Miller records. She often made it seem as if it were the two of us against the world.

In 1947, Ursula Burtner Kaufman married William Frohlich. The wedding didn't take place in the church, but in the chapel of the First Reformed Church of College Point. I remember the chapel and can recall the crowd of people at the house after the wedding. In my four-year-old brain, only one thing mattered; I had a daddy. So the natural thing to do was celebrate, which I did by running and skipping around the yard yelling, "I got a daddy!" Grandma Burtner heard me, rushed over, and grabbed me by the shoulder. She said, "Be quiet! Don't say that!" So I shut up, but I never could figure out why I wasn't allowed to be happy.

Bill was an only child, adopted. He had fought in the war in Europe as a Sergeant in the Army. He was a handsome man and, according to Mom, a great dancer. The Burtners did not much care for Bill; he didn't seem to have much ambition, and his prospects were not promising. I know this because they told me so, and very often, as I grew older. So it was decided that Ursula and

Daddy

Bill would begin married life without me. My grandparents sold the house and moved out of the city to a 103 acre spread on the side of a hill into a house that grandpa had built as a weekend getaway in Sullivan County in upstate New York. And I went with them.

The house was located on a country road between Calicoon Center and Jeffersonville, about a hundred and twenty-five miles from College Point. There was a long gravel drive straight up the hill from the road which led to the house Grandpa had built on the left. It was a plain white, one story, clapboard-sided structure with a dark roof and a front porch. To the right side of the drive was a small machine shed where Grandpa hoped to run his metal lathe and do side work as a tool and die maker. Further back to the right stood an old barn.

Behind the barn was an apple orchard and beyond that a cultivated field rented by a local farmer to grow a feed crop. To the right of the shed was a heavily wooded area. Somewhere in there was a stream, clear and sparkling, meandering through the trees. I remember picking winter greens there with Mom that Christmas, when she came to visit.

Standing next to the house, looking back down the drive, you could see the land dropped sharply down away from the road. As the land rose again, you could see a school in the distance, red brick with white pillars. The road curved in from the south from Jeffersonville, ran straight by the house, then turned north toward Calicoon Center. Near the house was an open well with a built-up stone rim. Grandpa once whistled loudly and scared a big snake out of the gaps in the stones.

Mom would visit occasionally. Sometimes we'd go to Jeffersonville or Libertyville for ice cream. Coffee was my favorite flavor. We once attended a county fair, and I remember seeing farm tractors square dancing, rising up on their rear wheels. Sometimes Grandma and Grandpa would go to Calicoon Center where there was a General Store with a big dog. I once petted that dog and said, "nice cow." You can take the kid out of the city, but you can't take the city out of the kid.

There was a cat that lived there on the hill with us and there may have been a dog, but mostly I remember the goat. Why Grandpa bought a goat I'll never know, but I adopted it as my pet. Using ropes, I tried to hitch it to my wagon to pull me around (one goat-power wheels!). We played every day until one day they told me the goat was sick, and they took it away.

I remember that winter it snowed. A lot. The winter of 1947–48 was a record-breaker. The farmer came around with his team of horses to help dig us out. The snow was well over my head and pretty far up on the

Daddy

horses too. That winter caused Grandpa to regret moving upstate and led to his decision to move back to the city the next summer.

I was free to wander all over this wonderful place, although I'm certain I did not venture too far from sight of the house. There was little traffic on the road, and there were no neighbors. There are photos showing Mom and Bill visiting at Christmas, and some of a picnic outside with Bill's parents, Fred and Emma Frohlich. There are pictures of me on skis, posing with a twenty-two rifle, and me and the goat. But I recall none of these events. I was four years old when we moved there and five when we left about a year later.

I cannot remember one thing about the inside of that house. I cannot remember one meal we ate in that house. I don't remember feeling anything, except happy when I played outside with that goat.

"Train up a child in the way he should go; even when he is old he will not depart from it."
Proverbs 22:6 ESV

Chapter 4

A FAMILY

I never learned how to play. In fall 1948, Mom and Bill (now Dad) enrolled me in the first grade at Public School (PS) 29 in College Point. Because of my birthdate, I was too old for kindergarten and barely old enough for first grade. Someone decided that it was okay for me to skip the playtime and socializing and get right into the real learning stuff. This meant that for the next twelve years, I'd always be younger than most of my classmates. So, after spending a whole year in the company of two old people and having no contact with any other child, I was inserted into a pre-existing social order. I had no clue, and I became too shy and too serious. What's more, now I had

A Family

a new name, Robert William Frohlich. Of course, at the age of five, I didn't really know or care much about last names. My birth name was unknown to me; all I knew was the new name I had been given. To my grandparents I was Bobby. Mom called me Bob. And the teacher called me Robert.

Now I was a student, living in a home with a mom and a dad, and that same September in 1948, my brother John was born. Seemingly, I took it all in stride, but my little boy head must have been spinning with all the changes.

But none of this was as life changing as was the fact that Dad was a member of the First Reformed Church and that I began to attend Sunday School. "Jesus Loves Me, This I Know" and flannel board stories began to take hold in my mind and heart. Through eighth grade I had perfect attendance, including the after-school Catechism classes. We got out of school early on Wednesdays to attend those classes. I was always jealous of my Catholic friends because they got out early for two years, while we Protestants enjoyed just one year of early release.

The stories about Moses, King David, Daniel, Joseph and Mary, and Jesus told though colorful cutouts on the flannel board brought the characters to life. The Sunday School teachers were all patient and kind.

My favorite was Mrs. Grace Johnson. She was a beautiful lady who spoke softly with a Midwestern tinge to her voice. Her smile and gentleness made a lasting impression on me.

While God was building a spiritual foundation in me, of which I was mostly unaware, I was setting my sights on joining the Emanon Society, the church youth group for high school kids. They were so grown up. They had their own meetings, they had Saturday night socials with music and dancing, they put on plays, and once a year they led the Youth Sunday Service. That became my objective: grow up and join the Emanons. But first, I had a childhood to endure.

Years later, a high school counselor would call me an underachieving intellectual tramp. I got started on that early. My God-given intellect allowed me to get good grades without having to work at it much. Everything came easy, so I made no effort to excel. I was happy to get As because it made Mom and Dad happy, and it pleased my grandparents who had great expectations for me. Basically, I day dreamed my way through grade school. I had no friends until the later years, but no conflicts either. I was content to play alone, as my little brother, John, was still too young to play with me, or ride my wagon, scooter, or roller skates up and down the hill on 26th Avenue where we lived. This began my great love for

A Family

wheels as a means of escape. It always felt good to be alone, to be able to wander wherever I pleased.

Our sister, Joanne, was born in 1951, and we had become a typical family. Mom, Dad, and three kids, living on the ground floor of a two-family house, the last house on a dead end street. Dad went to work every day and Mom mostly stayed home, except when she worked part-time at Gertz Department store in Flushing. We didn't have a lot of money. Dad drove an unimpressive old Plymouth.

The house on 26th Avenue was at the bottom of a hill that ended where a sandy marshland began. The sandy part became a wonderful playground. I could picture I was out west somewhere, riding my (imaginary) horse through the sagebrush. It was mostly cattails and weeds, but to me it was Wyoming.

There were only nine houses on the block. Directly across the street lived an old Irishman who grew vegetables in his backyard. I remember sneaking into the garden and snatching a few green beans off the vine. They were delicious. There were two more houses next to his, and the house on the corner was very neat and buttoned up. I understood somehow that that property was off limits, and I don't recall ever seeing the people who lived there.

Next door on our side of the street lived a policeman and his wife who had a son about my age named George. He must have attended a parochial school because we were never schoolmates and rarely playmates. The next house I remember was where the Italian-Irish family lived. It was a large, two-story brick home and the entire front yard was paved in concrete and surrounded by a white picket fence with brick and concrete pillars at the corners. The Italian grandfather was a retired mason contractor. He had recreated a Mediterranean villa complete with fig trees in the backyard. The Irish son-in-law and wife had a daughter, Nancy, who was about my age and a frequent playmate. The other child in the home was her cousin Ginny, who was about the same age as my brother, John.

On our side of the street, all the lots dropped sharply down from the street toward the wet, marshy area, a vast expanse that was slowly being filled with refuse from the long line of city garbage trucks that came in behind us every day. The drop off was severe enough that the basement was nearly fully exposed at the rear of all the houses, and the free-standing garage at the end of the driveway was built on stilts at the rear. It was under our garage that I once tried to grow my own garden and where I smoked my first cigarette.

A Family

In our yard was an old wooden rowboat, well-settled and rotting to become one with the earth. I made it into my Flash Gordon spaceship ready for traveling the stars as the brave space pioneer. There was a small shed for no apparent purpose. Dad locked me in it once as punishment for some misdeed. Farther back there were some trees and soft, spongy ground. One of the larger trees had fallen over sometime in the past and now, with its roots exposed, it stuck out into space at about a thirty-degree angle.

The tree provided great fun. I would scramble up the base of the trunk and work my way up until I was straddling the tree high up in the air. One cold, gray day, John, Ginny, and I were playing back there. John was too small to make the initial climb up the trunk, so I put my young cowboy/space cadet mind to work and tried to apply the rudimentary laws of physics to get John up there with me. I got a rope and tied one end around John's chest, under his arms, then threw the other end of the rope up over the trunk to a notch about six feet above the ground. Then, not having the strength to pull John up into the tree, I decided to use my weight advantage. I scampered up the trunk and tied a loop in the end of the rope and inserted my cowboy-booted foot into said loop. The plan was simple. I would let myself down on one side of the trunk thereby hoisting hapless John so he could share in the great experience of being up high. Then I slipped.

I fell off my side of the trunk, grabbing for something to hang onto and finding nothing but air. Gravity being what it is caused me to wind up, head down, suspended by one foot, dangling in the air. Meanwhile, John on the other side of the trunk was also suspended in the air, clad in his puffy winter jacket with his arms straight out on either side, the rope tight around his chest. Ginny was laughing hysterically.

"Go get my mom!" I screamed at Ginny. I can only imagine Mom's first thought when she beheld one son dangling by a rope around his chest and the other upside down dangling by his foot. Years later, Mom would laugh at the memory of that sight.

During the summer, the iceman would come, delivering ice to those who did not yet have an electric refrigerator. We kids would gather at the back of his wagon, and he'd chip off a chunk of ice for each of us, a cool delight in the heat of August. Others would come, like the knife sharpener in his wagon receiving dull knives from the mothers and returning them renewed for service in the kitchen and the man who brought a horse and sold rides to the kids. Of course, there was the ice cream man. We'd all mob him for our ice cream in a cup with chocolate

A Family

on top and a wooden spoon. Milk was delivered early in the morning, left in the box on our front stoop. The bakery man would stop by every week or so, bringing cakes to our door. Maybe he brought bread too, but I only remember the cakes: rich devil's food with creamy sweet white frosting.

In winter, when we had enough snow, we'd take our steel-runnered sleds to the hill above the intersection where our block began. The hill was a vacant lot on the corner. On a good day, with the snow packed just right, you could do a running belly flop onto the sled and race down the hill, across the sidewalk, across the street and right down the middle of our road to end up near our house. Fun for us, but Dad had to put chains on the rear wheels of the car so he could drive up the hill and go to work.

I walked to school every day, rain or shine, hot or cold. It was about ten blocks to PS 29, and I met schoolmates along the way. When lunchtime came, I'd walk back home, eat the sandwich Mom prepared, and trudge back to school to finish out the day, then walk home again.

Often, Mom would send me to the grocery store about four blocks away. The usual list would include a loaf of bread, sliced ham for sandwiches, and a pack of Pall Mall cigarettes.

It was mostly a peaceful life. But sometimes it wasn't. One time, a cigar-smoking insurance man came to the house to collect the monthly premium. He walked right into the kitchen, unannounced, since we didn't lock the doors back then. Mom threw him out. We didn't have the money.

Our upstairs neighbors were an old couple of sad alcoholics. They'd throw things around, stomp their feet, and yell at each other. One day, the old man came down the steps yelling about me roller skating in the hallway. He and Dad had a great row.

Sometimes Mom and Dad would quarrel. She did most of the yelling. One time, Mom threw an ashtray at Dad. She missed, but took a big chunk out of the plaster around the chimney in the kitchen.

Unlike my grandparent's house in the country, I can recall everything about this house. The kitchen was a large square room. There was a wall-hung sink and drain board on the inside wall and next to that the Frigidaire washing machine. It was unique in that instead of an agitator that swished the clothes from side to side, it worked up and down making a thump, thump sound. The gas stove was the old fashioned kind that stood on legs, with open burners on top. The table and chairs were fifties chrome, with a blue table top and blue seat cushions. They sat by the double window overlooking the driveway. The refrigerator and cupboards occupied the remaining wall.

Off of the kitchen to the rear of the house were two doors leading to the two bedrooms. The one to the left was Mom and Dad's. The one on the right contained the twin beds for John and me. Off to one side of our room was another small room stuck to the side of the house, supported by pillars. It was very cold in that room in the winter. At first, it was our play room; later, it became our sister's nursery.

Entry into the house was through a front door into a long hallway, with French doors to the left that led into our living room. At the end of the hall to the left was the stairway to the old couple's flat. Directly ahead was the door that opened into the kitchen. From the kitchen to the left was a small alcove with a storage closet. To the right was the bathroom, to the left was the living room, and directly ahead was another stuck-on room on stilts that served as our pantry. The living room had a couch, an upright piano, and a large radio/record player. The floor in the whole house was covered in variously colored linoleum.

There was a basement, but I didn't spend much time there, except for the time I filled a shallow aquarium with water and tadpoles I'd scooped up out of the swamp. I sort of forgot about them until one day, Dad found baby toads hopping about the basement. So ended my aspirations to be a wildlife curator and maybe explains why I spent punishment time in that shed in the back yard.

Life on the block was mostly good, and school was mostly easy, if somewhat boring. Sometime around eighth grade, I started smoking, not every day, but just enough to let my rebel side out. I always carried matches with me even though I did not always have cigarettes. One day in spring 1956, we were standing in line in the classroom, waiting to be dismissed for lunch. I started fooling with the matches, lighting them one at a time, then flicking them to the floor where they went out. Just showing off. One match went into the coat closet.

I went home, ate my sandwich, and walked back to school. As I approached the school yard, all the students were lined up outside, and there were fire engines everywhere. My carelessly tossed match, which I had supposed was out like the others, had instead landed still lit on the oiled wood floor of the closet, where it smoldered in the dust as we marched happily to lunch.

Fortunately, the damage was limited to the coat closet, and no one was hurt. The classroom was unusable for a time, and we were placed in another room. My heart was in my throat. Naturally, all the students

A Family

were questioned, but the culprit was not revealed.

Eventually I confessed twice. I was in woodworking class the next day and couldn't stand the guilt. I asked my friend Ray to come with me, and together we went to the principal's office where I confessed. The reaction was shock. I was scheduled to be valedictorian at the upcoming eighth grade graduation ceremonies, an honor student despite my lack of effort. Now I was going to court. That night after I went to bed, I called Mom into my room and said, "Mom, I started that fire at school." "How did you do that?" she asked. "What were you doing with matches?"

Dad, while driving me to court simply said, "That was a stupid thing to do." The fire marshal questioned me, mostly to determine if I was "fascinated by fire" or just stupid. He was convinced; I was stupid. Before the hearing in the courtroom, Dad said that I should respond to the judge's (hopefully) favorable verdict by raising my right hand in the Boy Scout salute and saying, "On my honor, I will do my best!" I didn't do that. The judge also asked if I was a pyromaniac or just stupid, and he came to the same conclusion as the Fire Marshall. I was let off with a stern warning to stay away from matches. I was placed on some sort of probation, but, barring any further trouble, my record would be sealed, and no punishment would be forthcoming.

The way I'd been brought up taught me that being "good" meant not embarrassing the family. Although I coveted my family's approval, impressing other people did not seem to be a great reason for not misbehaving. So, every now and then, I'd do something just to break the monotony of constantly being patted on the head like a good puppy.

I was not valedictorian at graduation; some girl got the honor. Mom and my eighth grade teacher had a good cry about my fallen state. I thank God that no one was hurt in the fire. In a final irony, while at scout camp the following year, I flunked the test to earn my Fire Maker badge.

> "...the Lord Jesus Christ, who gave himself for our sins to deliver us from the present evil age, according to the will of our God and Father, to whom be the glory forever and ever."
> Galatians 1:4 ESV

Chapter 5

A GOOD SCOUT

Joining the Cub Scouts was not my idea. Dad had been a Scout as a boy and was determined that I should have the same good experience. At the age of eight in 1951, I joined Cub Pack 20, sponsored by the First Reformed Church. Dad and Mom joined too. It was great fun. I got the whole dark blue uniform and bright yellow bandana. In three years, I earned every rank and every badge, even to the Cub Scout pinnacle of Webelos. I still have all those badges, carefully preserved in an album Mom created. Then it was on to Boy Scout Troop 20, where the pace to rank and achievement slowed considerably. I was less focused on earning approval and more interested in having fun and enjoying new adventures. The hikes and camping trips were great adventures (except for that one failure to start a fire). Growing up, learning to be a good scout, being built up in character and self-sufficiency were all good things. I learned survival skills, tested myself against the other boys, and learned to be more independent. We took long hikes, and when other boys would slow up and complain, I'd relish the walk and the new places we'd get to see. I owe a lot to scouting.

Then one evening, after a troop meeting, I went to the bathroom in the church basement. An assistant scout leader followed me in. He was in his late twenties, much bigger and stronger than I was. As I was about to leave, he began to molest me. It was sickening and terrifying. I didn't know what to do. I felt ashamed, confused, and horrified. Then he wanted to unzip my pants. I refused to let him and he began to twist my arm. We struggled for a while and he finally gave up saying, "Boy, when you don't want to do something, you really don't want to do it!" Those were his exact words; I never forgot them. We left the church basement and went outside and stood on the sidewalk. "Don't tell anyone about this, okay?" he said. I nodded and asked for a cigarette. I was thirteen years old. I never told anyone.

A Good Scout

I grew bored with Boy Scouts, so at the age of fourteen I joined the local Air Explorer Post, led by a man named Ed Bonn Jr. The Scout Explorer programs had a more interest-based focus, and were designed for older boys. We wore cool powder blue uniforms and marched in parades as color guard, aviation sunglasses and all. Most of the guys were older than I was. We met at Flushing Airport, a small commercial strip that I could see from my house on 26th Avenue. Skywriters were based out of this airport, and I loved to watch them take off, fly high in the air, and write "Pepsi Cola" in white smoke against the blue summer sky.

Our meetings consisted of learning a little about airplanes, but our fun came from parades, camping, and shooting. We would shoot at an indoor rifle range in the basement of the Poppenhusen Institute. One night, Ed's youngest son, Joe (who was too young to be in our troop), was shooting with us. There were four or five lanes in the semi-dark basement. Each shooting station was separated by a wooden partition. We shot from a prone position using bolt action 22 caliber rifles. I had just sat up to reload when Joe in the station to my right also sat up to unjam his rifle. He held the rifle across his knees and hit the bolt. The rifle fired. The bullet went right through the partition at about the same location where my head had been just a moment before. I hadn't had much to do with Joe prior to that night, but from there on I deliberately avoided him. I eventually came to like his father, Ed, even less.

Eventually, my interest in girls overwhelmed my interest in scouting, so I quit. Mom was upset because she felt I still needed to be with other young males, but the siren call of lovely young ladies in angora sweaters was too powerful to ignore.

"If you confess with your mouth that Jesus is Lord and believe in your heart that God raised him from the dead, you will be saved."
Romans 10:9 ESV

Chapter 6

SAVED

Growing up in the Reformed Church, I was exposed to very sound doctrine through very careful teaching. The people around me were good, serious Christians. Our Sunday School was filled with eager and earnest teachers. Every Sunday when all the students gathered in assembly, one of the black-suited elders would stand up in front to greet and exhort us. On the walls of the chapel where we met were scripture verses written large in elegant colored script. Invariably we would sing a hymn such as "My Faith Looks Up To Thee." Then the elder would quote from Psalm 51:

"Have mercy on me, O God, according to thy lovingkindness; according to the multitude of thy tender mercies blot out my transgressions. Wash me thoroughly from mine iniquity and cleanse me from my sin."

"Against thee, thee only have I sinned and done this evil in thy sight, that thou mightiest be justified when thou speakest and be clear when thou judgest."

"Restore unto me the joy of thy salvation; and uphold me with thy free spirit, then will I teach transgressors thy ways; and sinners shall be converted unto thee." (Psalm 51:1–2, 4, 12–13 KJV)

The elder would then expound on how marvelously we were made, created in God's own image. We traipsed off to our individual classrooms to absorb the lesson of the day. I cannot tell you how vitally important these lessons were, gradually building in me the very foundation of faith, so that when the spirit moved, my heart would be ready. The way Jesus was depicted, teaching and healing ordinary people, forever changing their lives just by His presence made a lasting impression on me. The Son of God came down to be with His people and to save them.

In eighth grade, we attended weekly catechism classes on Wednesday afternoons with the pastor, Reverend Harold Klein. Following my usual lazy path, when Reverend Klein told us up front which questions we'd be asked by the elders in June, I dutifully crossed out all the questions we would not be asked. We used an abbreviated version of the catechism, and the lessons weren't too hard. We were expected to attend worship regularly, preparing ourselves to become full communicant members by the end of the school year.

In June 1956, I sat before the pastor and elders, answered the questions, and became a full member of the church, meeting all expectations. My status had changed but my heart was still the same.

My dream of joining the Emanon Society was finally realized in 1956. Upon entering high school, I was now eligible to join the church youth group and to come under the influence of two wonderful people, Donald and Ella Plitt. Ella was the heart and soul of the youth group, patiently leading our bi-weekly meetings on Sundays and our bi-weekly socials on Saturdays. She prayed over us like a mother. She wrote simple musical plays using popular music, which we performed each year. Everyone in the church and many other friends and relatives bought tickets to our performances. The proceeds went toward funding summer camping opportunities at one of our Reformed Church camps. Don was her strength and support, always there, always smiling, willing to do whatever was needed to make Emanons a good growing experience for us. I admired the older kids, like Don and Ella's son, Dan, who could smoothly lead a meeting or conduct a devotional. And I was in awe of the older girls, so beautiful, so confident, so good, and so way out of my league.

The Emanons became my way of life for the next four years. My friend Ray and I were constant companions, having gone through grade school and confirmation class together. I became friends with Dan Plitt and Lou Jones, who were college age but still connected with the group. It was fun, it was safe, and it was crucial to my survival during those high school years.

At Flushing High School, I did my classwork and nothing else. I rode the orange line city bus to Flushing, attended classes, and retuned home. I never went to a game, played a sport, attended a social event, or did anything there except go to class. There were about four thousand students in the school, and when I graduated in 1960, there were eight hundred fifty-three in my class. I knew very few of them and had exactly one friend, Ray.

In spring 1957, Billy Graham came to New York City. He was a powerful evangelist who conducted large revival meetings in cities all over the world. His message was simple and direct: Christ died for our sins, and we need to decide to receive the gift of eternal salvation. His team rented Madison Square Garden, the famous sports arena in Manhattan, and began the New York Crusade for Christ on May 15. The Crusade was scheduled to last six weeks. But because of the tremendous response and the urging of church leaders in the city, the Crusade was extended and extended and extended again until it ended after sixteen weeks in a final rally in Times Square on September 1, 1957.

Don and Ella Plitt began singing in the Crusade choir, and Dan and Lou helped out in other ways. I attended once and was impressed with Mr. Graham's direct presentation of the gospel, the large crowds—numbering about eighteen thousand each night—filling the Garden, and the beautifully-voiced, fifteen-hundred-member choir under the direction of Cliff Barrows, the Crusade music director. At the end of the message, Mr. Graham invited people to come and confess their faith publically by walking down to the front of the platform, where he would pray with them. I didn't go, but a seed of longing began to grow in my heart.

Life went on that summer, and that seed grew quietly until one Saturday morning I was at the bus stop in front of my grandparents' house. Dan Plitt drove up in his 1952 Ford convertible with the top down. "Hey, we're going to see Billy Graham again tonight. Want to go with us?" I said, "sure," and that was that. It was August 31, 1957, the very last night Mr. Graham would preach in the Garden.

It was the same crowd, the same beautiful choir, and the same powerful preaching of the gospel. I do not remember one word that Mr. Graham spoke, but I do recall the large banner above the platform that proclaimed, "Jesus said, I am the way, the truth and the life." At the end, when the invitation was given and with the choir softly singing "Just as I Am, Without One Plea," I looked at my friends indicating that I wanted to go. They smiled gently and nodded as I turned to make the long trek from high up in the arena to the front of the platform. There were tears in my eyes as I confessed my sin and received God's gift of salvation in Christ Jesus. I prayed a prayer of confession and was given some bible study and scripture memory cards. Mr. Graham encouraged us to get to a church on Sunday to begin our journey as newborn Christians.

Saved

When I returned home late that night, Mom was still awake. "I've been born again!" I said and told her everything that had happened. She told me years later that my face was shining that night. I had been in the presence of the Living God, convicted by the Holy Spirit and saved by the blood of the Lamb, Jesus. This was and is the biggest save that God ever worked in my life. Nothing would ever be the same after that night. But the struggles had only just begun.

A year later, my friend Lou presented me with a fine, leather-bound Bible. On the presentation page he wrote, "To Bob Frohlich, by Lou Jones, on the occasion of his first re-birthday, August 31, 1958." While working at another Billy Graham Crusade in San Francisco, Lou had Mr. Graham and the whole team sign the blank first page, front and back. I treasure that Bible to this very day.

"The Lord will fulfill his purpose for me;
your steadfast love, O Lord, endures forever.
Do not forsake the work of your hands."
Psalm 138:8 ESV

Chapter 7

THE BEST AND WORST OF TIMES

So began my journey as a confessed Christian. I was hungry to hear more of the gospel, eager to grow in faith and in service, enthusiastic about life and my future. I wanted to be Billy Graham. I wanted to be like him, preaching the gospel with power. "The Bible says..." was his most frequently used expression. It was never about Mr. Graham; it was always about Jesus. I read books written by Mr. Graham and books written about him. I listened to him on the radio. Like him, I wanted to share with others the great truth that Jesus saves.

The Best and Worst of Times

I assumed a leadership role in the Emanon Society. In 1959, I preached on Youth Sunday. I even preached a sermon at another church in town, at an evening service. I'm guessing it was forgettable because they never invited me back. I started teaching Sunday School and attended youth rallies and camps. By working hard and doing good things I thought I could become something and earn God's favor, which, of course, was already mine as a free gift.

I attended Summer Youth Camp twice. Unlike the Boy Scout camps that focused on outdoor skills and nature study, the Youth Camp experience was more about faith-building and fun in a very peaceful setting. Experienced counselors would help us think through our faith during fireside group discussions and private sessions. We spent a lot of time thinking about the future, how we might serve God in the years ahead. I was determined to serve God by becoming a minister.

While at camp, we were instructed to write a letter, addressed to ourselves. The letter was to be mailed out months later, in December. In 1958 I wrote in part:

> "You made a vow and you're going to keep it. Nothing must stand in your way. Don't worry about being popular, about having a girl, about what

people less fortunate than yourself think or if you are treated badly. You are Christ's and He is yours He will never fail you. Being a Christian is a wonderful thing, don't forget that. Having eternal life is God's most precious gift. Live it, love it, be kind, have patience, think, read the bible, help others, pray, worship, give and be. Study, learn, strive to succeed in being a minister." "Don't fail yourself or your God. Remember, it's not your life, it's God's. Serve Him."

In 1959, the letter was much shorter, and I wrote:

"A lot has happened this week. It was a joyous spiritual experience. I hope everything that was started here has grown. Have you helped? There's not much to say, but just remember, you'll never be perfect. Never feel higher than someone else. You're nothing. Anything you are or have is because God gave it to you. Remember to pray for others. They, like yourself, need God's help. Don't let God or them down."

Yet, I was still a teenage boy. Girls were always on my mind. They were fun to

The Best and Worst of Times

dance with, and my overly romantic soul kept falling in love, generally with girls who were too old for me or those who weren't interested. The few times I actually dated someone, it was sweet bliss just to hold her hand and Fourth of July fireworks whenever I actually kissed her. I dated a girl named Jane for a while. She was new in town, having moved up from somewhere in the south. It was fun to be with her the first time she experienced snow. She even gave me an engraved friendship bracelet. Then one day she tearfully told me there was someone else. Deeply hurt, I was walking home with my friend Ray. "Do you want to know who it was?" he asked. "It was me." I angrily ripped off the bracelet and threw it into some bushes. I told Ray it was okay and continued on home. After all, you can't end an enduring friendship for just some girl.

Wheels were always my way of escape. On 26th Avenue it had been my wagon and scooter. Then I graduated to roller skates and finally a new bike my grandparents gave me. I went everywhere on that bike, clocking mile after mile around town. I abused that bike, maybe because it wasn't "cool" enough. I sold it to a neighbor kid and told my grandparents it had been stolen. There was an old bike in Grandpa Frohlich's garage that I tore apart, cleaned and lubricated, and painted black. I built sort of a flat seat over the rear wheel and painted my name on it with white paint. This bike was truly mine, reconditioned and customized. Ray had a new "English Racer" with a three-speed shifter. We'd ride everywhere together, enjoying the speed, visiting girls, and showing off. I could ride for blocks with no hands, even turning corners. The freedom, the speed, and the independence were exhilarating. I would put my sister, Joanne, on the crossbar and take her to dancing lessons and watch her learn to "tap, tap, step."

Brother John got a new bike, a nice green Schwinn. I could ride my bike and pull his alongside, to take it to him at school so we could ride home together. One day, John and I were riding in the school yard of PS 129, John's school. Another boy was there and challenged John to a race. The idea was to start at the school building, ride to the fence, and return. I stayed behind to determine the winner. Off they went, peddling as hard as they could. Honest and earnest John rode all the way to the fence, but the other boy turned around far short. I was yelling as loud as I could, "Come on Johnny, you can still beat him!" The other boy arrived first, but John kept going, full speed, right into the brick wall. He hit the wall with his chin, which split open and started bleeding profusely. The other boy quickly departed. I knew I couldn't take John home like that.

The Best and Worst of Times

Mom would freak out, I thought. Instead, I took him to his Sunday School teacher's house a few blocks away. Mrs. Davis came to the door, and I asked her to help me clean John up a bit, which she did. Then I took John and his bike home. Mom looked at the wound and decided John needed a doctor. So I loaded him onto my bike and took him to see Dr. Spring on Main Street. The good doctor cleaned him up and applied a butterfly bandage. Then I took John back home. I hope that my heroics that day made up for the time when I almost hanged him.

Things were coming apart at home. I didn't see it, but I could sense it. Our family had moved out of the flat on 26th Avenue and into the Burtner's house on 7th Avenue. We had our own kitchen and living room in the basement, and on the second floor were bedrooms for Grandpa and Grandma, Mom and Dad, and Joanne. John and I slept in the attic which was accessible via a stairway with a landing halfway up where the stairway reversed direction. You had to duck the low ceiling to get up there. The room was quite large, with two twin-sized beds and a marble-topped desk. It was hot in the summer and cold in the winter, but we were comfortable enough. My grandparents had never much cared for Dad. And our moving in with them must have been caused by some financial crisis that only confirmed in their minds that Bill was not worthy of their daughter or their precious grandson, Bobby.

Bill's parents owned a two-family house on 115th Street. Bill was an adopted and only child, and I like to think that he adopted me and gave me his name out of gratitude to God. It must have been hard for him to have me around and especially difficult when I resisted his parenting. I disappointed him too. He always wanted me to become an Eagle Scout, but I wasn't interested, and it hurt him. Bill progressed from being an assistant leader in my troop through many leadership positions until he ultimately became the commissioner of scouting for Queens County. For his tireless work in scouting and his many years of service, he was awarded the Silver Beaver, which I believe is the highest honor scouting can bestow. He was a good man. My grandparents were dead wrong about him.

The two-family house owned by Bill's parents was also occupied by Bill's aunt Otillie Frohlich on the second floor. After Fred Frohlich had a stroke that left him unable to speak and partially paralyzed, Bill persuaded his aunt to move out. In 1958, we moved in. Now my mother had to not only care for her husband and children, but also watch over her invalid father-in-law and her rapidly failing mother-in-law, who

The Best and Worst of Times

descended into dementia after she broke her hip and was confined to a wheelchair.

Bill had a lot of work done on the house. New heating was installed, and he hired painters to do the outside. One of the painters was Ed Bonn III, son of my former scoutmaster Ed Jr. The family painted the inside a light gray with white trim. I was involved, but I wasn't very good at it; Dad kept telling me to "Put some paint on it!"

Grandpa Frohlich's old 1939 Chevy was in the garage. I had the battery charged at the gas station across the street and got the car started. Then, when no one was around, I'd take the car out and drive up and down the street. Actually, since it was a one-way street, I'd back it down the street to a factory parking lot and drive it around there. One day, I took John and had him drive it in the parking lot, though he could hardly reach the pedals. Poor Grandpa Frohlich would see all this from the front window. When I came back into the house he was agitated, and—struggling to get the words out—said, "Get insurance!"

Every now and then, I noticed my old scoutmaster Ed Jr.'s car parked in front of the house, and I just knew something was wrong. I mentioned it to Lou, who said, "Now Robert, they are adults after all, and it's none of your concern."

Then one day I was home alone with Mom, and the doorbell rang. Mom said "Oh, it's Grandma." And sure enough her mother came rushing up the stairs. She went straight to Mom, arms outstretched, and said, "I'm going to kill you!" I stepped between them and said, "What are you, stupid? You can't say something like that to my mother!" She was shocked; I had never spoken to her like that before.

After she left, I asked Mom what that was all about. She told me she was leaving Dad to be with Ed. I walked out and went to the garage, lit up a cigarette, and fumed. Anger was my way of dealing with life, and I punched my fist through the garage window and cut my hand. Instead of going to God for help, I mostly wanted to hurt the people who were hurting me. It seemed the only way to hurt them was to hurt myself. I was a senior in high school, planning to go to college the following year. Now my family was falling apart and my future was in doubt.

Mom and Ed moved to New Jersey. One day she was just gone. That night, I could hear Dad sobbing in his bed. The next day, I helped get John and Joanne ready for school. I brushed Joanne's long blond hair and tried to arrange it so she'd look nice at school.

That weekend, I went to our youth meeting. Outside the church I talked with

The Best and Worst of Times

my friend Bob Zittel from Emanons and told him what was going on. We had worked on youth projects together and hung out with Lou Jones in his TV repair shop. I cried and said I didn't know where I was going to live now. He said, "Maybe you can live with us."

One school day, John and Joanne did not come home. Joanne, years later, told me that Mom and Ed showed up and took them out of school. Mom took them home to pack, and when they got back into the car, she pointed to Ed and said, "From now on, you call him Dad." They headed off to New Jersey.

So now it was just Dad and me. He was devastated. I was sad, angry, and confused. Late one night, I decided to do what my family had taught me to do: run away. I didn't pack, I just slipped out of the house and walked to the bus stop. I thought I'd go to New Jersey and visit a girl named Jan who I'd met at summer camp. The bus took me to Flushing where I got on the subway train to Manhattan and the Port Authority Terminal. It was an enormous building, the transportation hub for New York City. Here, the subway trains connected with the intercity busses and the national railways. Around the perimeter of the great main hall were ticket windows, coffee shops, gift shops, smoke shops, and places to eat. It was busy day and night.

I found a bench and sat down, contemplating my next move. It was around midnight. Suddenly, a young man approached me and said, "Hey, you want to come to a party? Come on, it'll be fun." I was stunned and repulsed by this undesirable invitation and just shook my head no. It came to me then that I was in a very dangerous place, sixteen and all alone. If I were to persist in this journey there was no telling how it might end. So I decided to go back home, such as it was. I boarded the subway to Flushing, took the bus back home, and crept into bed around two in the morning. The next day I went to school.

I went to see Reverend Klein at the First Reformed Church. I was heartbroken, and I said to him, "But divorce is wrong!" He responded, "Not in the case of adultery." Given the circumstances, I told him I'd quit teaching Sunday School. There was just too much shame. I felt ashamed of my family and took the failure on myself, not that it was my fault. It just seemed that I was no longer worthy to be a teacher because of the circumstances. Reverend Klein did not disagree, and I don't recall him offering any comfort. In fact, he said I was a most unstable individual.

It was Christmas time, and I went to Bob Zittel's house one night. His mother, Kay, presented me with a small wrapped package.

The Best and Worst of Times

When I unwrapped it, it was a small jewelry box. Inside was a house key and a note that said, "Just in case." On this Earth, it was the greatest gift I had ever received; an invitation to shelter and family and love when I was most in need.

Decisions were made. I would not go with Mom because I detested Ed, and I wanted to finish my last semester in my own school. My grandparents were out because they were angry. Dad was out because he had too much to deal with caring for his parents in a newly empty home. I moved in with Bob, his younger sister Ruth, and his Mom and Dad, Kay and Charlie.

Arrangements were made to pay the Zittels ten dollars a week for food and board. I carried my laundry each week to Grandma Burtner. I slept in Bob's bed, and he slept on the sofa. How we remained friends during that semester I'll never know. Charlie was a character, and Kay was infinitely patient and loving. I was moody and unmotivated. I'd get frustrated with my homework and walk out of the house to wander aimlessly for a while, then return and finish the assignment. Bob and I were still active in the youth group, and he was now the leader. On Sunday evenings I'd go visit Don and Ella Plitt. We'd listen to Billy Graham on the radio then watch "Bonanza," the popular western family drama on television.

All these loving people showed me what family could and should be; they lived out their faith before me, nurturing me through this tough time in my life. They exhibited a hope in me that deep inside I did not feel for myself.

The semester was coming to a close. The school guidance counselor called me an "intellectual tramp" for my lack of effort because I just managed to make it into the top third of my eight-hundred fifty-three member graduating class. However, I had gained admission to a Reformed Church-affiliated school, Central College in Pella Iowa, where I planned to get a degree and then study for the ministry. Everyone agreed that was what I should do.

I was ambivalent about attending the graduation ceremonies but decided it was the easiest way to get my hands on the diploma. So, capped and gowned, I walked across the stage to get the thing, and to this day I can't recall who, if anyone, was there to see me grab it. A celebration was held at the Zittels' home afterwards. There is a photo me, gowned but cap-less, holding my Bible: a hopeful look toward an unknown future.

Two things caused me to move in with Mom and Ed that summer. It saved the ten bucks a week we were paying the Zittels, and Ed was going to get me a job at United Parcel Service where he worked and had some

The Best and Worst of Times

influence as a union steward. I filled out an application, lying about my age because I was only seventeen (you had to be eighteen to work there), and began my summer job as a delivery helper. We worked out of the Bloomingdale's warehouse in Hunters Point, Queens, delivering furniture and household goods for the big department store. The pay was two dollars an hour plus tips we received from many of the customers. Each day I was assigned to a driver to help load and deliver goods throughout New York City.

One day I was assigned to work with a wiry Italian guy who made it clear that he didn't want to work with some (expletive) college kid. He refused to talk to me except to grunt out an order when necessary. It was going to be a long day. About mid-morning we had a stop at a four story walk-up apartment. Checking the orders, I saw we had a large carpet going to the second floor and a full bedroom suite going to the fourth floor. I opened the back of the truck and grabbed the carpet, which was huge.

"What do you think you're doing?" shouted the driver.

"I'm going to deliver this carpet," I said.

He sneered and said, "If you can deliver that carpet then I'll deliver the whole bedroom set myself."

I hoisted the carpet onto my shoulder, staggered across the street and manhandled it into the hallway. The open stairway was split, with a landing halfway between each floor. I dragged the carpet up to the landing, then heaved it up over the railing, dragged it into the hall, and repeated the process. I knocked on the door of the apartment, but no one answered. I left the carpet in the hallway, stuck the paperwork in the door, went back downstairs, climbed into the cab of the truck, and sat there while the wiry Italian guy hauled the entire bedroom suite to the fourth floor. When he finished, he climbed up into the cab, turned to me, and said, "Wanna go get some coffee?"

All that summer, I traveled back and forth to College Point to be with my friends at church, worshiping and participating in youth group activities. On Saturday, July 4th, there was a beach party. We left the church and were driven to the beach by Don and Ella Plitt and others who had cars. It was a good day to be alive: sun, sand, salt water, and girls. Now, although I was not a swimmer, I was highly motivated when I decided to pursue one of the young lovelies into the water. She was an excellent swimmer, and I splashed madly along behind her, rapidly losing ground. Suddenly I grew tired and discovered I could not touch bottom. Since I'd never learned to float, I sank and I panicked. The sun made the water sparkle like diamonds, but I was going under, gasping

The Best and Worst of Times

for air and swallowing water. With my whole future just out there ahead of me, was I going to die? "Are you done with me already, God?" I prayed as I went down for the third time, consciousness fading fast.

Then I felt an arm around me, grabbing me from behind. I was pulled through the waves and dragged onto the beach. My friends later said I was gray, and they thought I was dead. The man who pulled me out walked away and disappeared. My stomach and lungs were filled with salt water. I slowly rolled over and vomited. An ambulance was summoned, and I was taken to a local hospital. It was all hazy and blurry. I gurgled when I breathed. The doctors wanted to admit me, to monitor my condition in case pneumonia set in. I refused, saying we couldn't afford the cost. They released me into the care of Don and Ella, who made the long drive to Weehawken, New Jersey to Mom's house. There, I gurgled for a couple of days and then went back to work. God, apparently, was not quite finished with me.

"Behold, I am with you and will keep you wherever you go, and will bring you back to this land. For I will not leave you until I have done what I have promised you."
Genesis 28:15 ESV

Chapter 8

Escape From New York

Off I went to Pella, Iowa in September 1960, riding with Dan Plitt, a senior at Central College. Riding with us was another senior named Ellen. I was ecstatic. At last I could escape my broken family and my own failure to deal with it all. College would provide me with the education I needed to get me into seminary. Using my verbal gifts, I'd become a pastor and perhaps a great preacher like Billy Graham. Leaving behind my grandparents' expectations to be their perfect grandson who would never bring shame to the family like their daughter did. Leaving behind my mother who was now in her third marriage and still not happy. Leaving behind a Dad who never really wanted me but did his best to raise me. Leaving it all behind to make my own way, I was ready to start living life on my own terms.

In those days, I knew and believed that my sins were forgiven in Christ alone, but my trust was incomplete. I felt it was all up to me now to fulfill the expectations of all those people in the church who wished me well, who were no doubt praying for me. It was up to me to overcome the trials of my childhood, to go on in my own strength and succeed despite my poor start in life. I had a lot to learn.

Pella, Iowa was a paradise, and Central College was a dream come true. The town was built around a town square park, where tulips would bloom in the spring. The population was about five thousand people, mostly of Dutch descent. Everything was neat, clean and tidy. On every other corner, it seemed, there was a Reformed Church. On the park-like square was a glassed-in bulletin board in which were displayed individual photos of the entire incoming freshman class at Central College. People said, "Hello!" when I walked down the street. It was quiet. On opposite ends of the town were two factories. One manufactured premium "Pella" windows and the other built digging machines, "Vermeer, The Digging Dutchman."

Outside the town were endless fields of corn, interspersed with pastures where Holstein milk cows grazed and muddy pens where pigs fed. Nowhere were there any smoking busses, noisy trains, honking horns or rude people. I would have been happy to drive around in those corn fields for the rest of my life, just to enjoy the peace.

The student body that year consisted of about four hundred twenty-five young people from all around the country. The campus was near the edge of town. Some of the buildings dated back to the school's founding in 1853, while others, like my dorm, were quite new. I shared a room with my friend Dan and another freshman, Tom. Everything was in easy walking distance: classrooms, chapel, dining hall, and the student union and cafeteria where, unfortunately, I was to spend more time than in class or studying.

Placement tests landed me in a small advanced English class that consisted mostly of writing essays on assigned books. Other classes were biology, sociology, and Old Testament survey. The writing class was fun. I started dating a girl named Yvonne who was also in the class. I began to see the possibility of a grown up future with an attractive and intelligent woman who was fun to be with.

We had other classes together. One day in sociology class, Yvonne asked how I had fared writing the essay that was due in the next class hour. She said she'd been up most of the night writing and rewriting and was nervous about the grade she might receive. I confessed that I'd forgotten the essay was due, and proceeded to write it right there in sociology class. A few days later, we got the graded essays back. Yvonne said she was relieved with the C grade she received, then asked what I got. When I told her I got an A, she would not speak to me for a couple of days.

The "intellectual tramp" label bestowed on me by the high school counselor proved to be prophetic. I exerted minimal effort in all my classes, resulting in As in English and a couple of Ds and an F in the others. Although they were included in my room and board, I often did not eat meals in the dining hall, spending summer job earnings on coffee and breakfast rolls in the union cafeteria and pizza burgers—a burger filled with sauce and topped with cheese—at a local joint in town. I quickly fell into a lazy, aimless way of life.

Once, we drove up to Des Moines to a pizza place called Babe's. It wasn't New York pizza, but it served as a good substitute.

The very next year, my future wife would come to work in Des Moines and also have pizza at Babe's. Midwest pizza may not be as good as New York's, but Babe's is special for other reasons.

On the night of the 1960 presidential election in November, the early returns showed Kennedy leading. I was a Nixon guy, for what reason I don't recall. Giving vent to my anger, I borrowed Dan's car and drove to town to get a pizza burger. And I drove fast. The town cop caught me doing about sixty on Main Street. Small town justice was about to descend on me.

The cop made his charges against me to the judge. The judge pronounced a sentence of sixty dollars or three days in jail. I said I couldn't afford the sixty bucks and asked if I could serve my three days in jail over Thanksgiving weekend. The judge asked when was I going home next, and I told him it would be at Christmas time. He took my license and locked it up in the town safe, saying I could pick it up before I went home for Christmas. He also told me to report for jail on the Friday after Thanksgiving.

For Thanksgiving, the local churches arranged for the out-of-town students to have Thanksgiving dinner with various local families. I was taken to a large farm house just outside of town, where I enjoyed a fine meal in the company of a very kind family.

It was a nice touch of grace before I went to jail.

Small town justice being what it was, they did not put me behind bars where I could languish and consider my sins. Instead, they put me to work. I was given a bucket, some rags, and a mop and told to thoroughly clean the public restrooms in the municipal building. Resupplying me with other cleaning solutions and devices, they pointed me to the two town patrol cars, ordering that they be washed and hand waxed. I worked about two and a half days and slept in my dorm room at night. And, of course, I walked everywhere until Christmas.

I began to have serious doubts about my call to ordained ministry. It seemed so hard to get motivated to do the necessary school work. I doubted my ability to provide leadership or comfort to a congregation. And I wasn't preaching.

Christmas break arrived, and after retrieving my driver's license, I spent my last few dollars on a bus ticket home, since Dan wasn't driving this time. I boarded a bus in Des Moines destined for Chicago, where another bus would take us to New York. Somewhere in Indiana, that second bus broke down. We sat in the cold and dark until another bus picked us up and took us to the next rest area. There we waited again until yet another bus picked us up and took us to New York. We were a little late getting in. I had a winter break job, working for United Parcel Service for about ten days to replenish my cash. I visited family and friends, then hurried back to Pella to finish out the first semester ending in January.

Upon returning to Pella, the first thing I did was buy a car. Now I rationalized it, of course (as I would rationalize the purchase of many of the thirty-six cars I have bought since then). First, Dan's car was unreliable because often it would not start in the cold weather. So my car would serve as sort of a mobile jump-start battery. Second, I wanted to be free to come and go without having to rely on Dan. What it was really about was freedom. I wanted to be free to come and go on my own terms, to not need anyone's help or permission, to go whenever and wherever I pleased.

It was a black 1949 two-door Ford—a rusty, worn out, oil burning nightmare that I bought for one hundred dollars. But the battery was good. It had a V-8 motor and a burned out muffler which made it sound more powerful than it was. It also had a manual transmission, which I didn't quite know how to operate and subsequently broke about a week into my ownership. It cost me twenty-five dollars to get the transmission replaced. I bought a case of cheap motor oil and put it in the trunk because the motor used about a quart of oil every fifty miles. But I was free!

I resumed not studying, and soon my birthday arrived on Friday, January 13. There was a quiet celebration. Yvonne brought a cake. It was 1961, and now I was eighteen. And eligible for the draft. And failing school. Party hats all around.

The following Monday, I got in the car having decided to go to a movie instead of attending class. As I drove, heading east, I thought, I have to register for the draft within five days of my birthday. My grandparents had given me three hundred dollars and my church had contributed sixty dollars for my education, and I was blowing it. I drove on. With final grades coming, I knew I'd receive a failing grade in one or two of my classes. I drove on. I couldn't see myself becoming what I thought God wanted me to be. Then I realized I was heading toward home. I stopped at a post office and mailed a postcard to Dan at school asking him to pack up my stuff and send it home. Continuing east, and stopping every fifty miles or so to pour in another quart of oil, I drove on into the evening. Somewhere in Indiana, my right front tire blew out. What was it with me and Indiana? After changing the tire, I found a garage that was still open and parted with more cash for two used tires, because the left front tire wasn't looking too good either.

I drove on, stopping once to call ahead to the Zittels' home. When Kay answered, I told her I was heading back and asked if I could stay there for a night. She said of course. After a long night of driving, I arrived in New York City, dirty, tired, and broke. And broken. I never said goodbye to Yvonne.

Naturally, everyone—my family, the Plitts, the Zittels, my friends—was upset. "What have you done?" "What will you do now?" "Why did you buy that car?" "Sell the car!" "Go back to school!"

On the fifth day after my eighteenth birthday, I went to the selective service office and registered for the draft. I offered to go into active service right then, but they couldn't take me for at least three months. So I walked a few blocks to the Army recruiter's office and enlisted. The sergeant asked what kind of training I wanted, and I said I didn't care. We settled on Chaplain's Assistant which sounded spiritual to me. He asked where I wanted to be stationed after training and I said Germany. He said I could be inducted the next day, but I asked for two weeks to settle things. Six months later I was in France. Still aimless.

"Yet he saved them for his name's sake, that he might make known his mighty power."
Psalm 106:8 ESV

Chapter 9

BIGGER WHEELS

The trip to Europe was on a troop ship, the USNS Buckner, where we were penned up like cattle for the ten-day voyage. I landed a job up top with the Chaplain so I got to spend some time enjoying the ocean view after I got my sea legs (and stomach). We landed in Bremerhaven, Germany, then boarded a train to Metz, France. From there, a bus took us to Etain, France. On the train, it was amazing to me to see the fatherland. The orderly cities, homes, and farms of Germany gave way to the less orderly, but charming landscape of France. Etain was home to a mothballed U.S. air base currently occupied by my new outfit, the 97th Engineer Battalion, Headquarters Company.

I was assigned to the base chapel and Chaplain Helsel, a very serious man with a trim moustache who held the rank of Colonel. The chapel was shared by a Catholic Chaplain (who was far more amiable than Colonel Helsel) and his assistant who showed me the ropes. It soon became apparent that being a chaplain's assistant had very little to do with faith and much to do with tedious, boring chores, one of which was preparing the weekly worship bulletin master for the mimeograph machine, which can best be described as a prehistoric copy machine. I did find time to pick out some of my favorite hymns on the piano during slack periods, but I soon felt trapped by this bad decision that I'd thoughtlessly made in haste back at the Army recruiter's office.

During the thirty-one months I was in France, I made two good friends. One was Tom Stickland, a tall lanky guy from Wisconsin who was the mail clerk. The other was a happy redhead from Washington, Mick Van Zandt, who became my Christian brother. He was a soils analyst. (This had nothing to do with hygiene in the barracks and everything to do with the load bearing capabilities of various types of earth.)

Shortly after I began my tour of duty, the Soviets erected the Berlin wall in August 1961, and the U.S strengthened its forces throughout Europe. Consequently, the

Bigger Wheels

Etain air base was re-activated and became occupied by a unit of the Ohio Air National Guard. The men who came were a little older and wiser than us GIs and a little bitter about being called up, giving up jobs, and leaving families to move to this remote area of France, waiting for the other shoe to drop. The 97th Engineer Battalion got kicked out and moved to the Sidi Brahim Caserne in the village of Etain.

By October that year, I had requested a change of duty and trained to be a heavy truck driver. They sent me away on temporary duty to drive a dump truck on a road building project in a munitions depot near the village of Vassincourt. We drivers and equipment operators bunked in Quonset huts and went to work each day just like a real job. The post we were on was staffed by Polish Army guardsmen. We couldn't converse with them, but we could enjoy their company at the post bar in the evening.

My first day of work was a Saturday. I drove the dump truck down into the water-filled gravel pit where a big bucket excavator overloaded the truck with wet sandy gravel. I was told to follow another truck, and off we went driving several miles through the countryside and a small village with narrow streets where sugar beets were piled high in front of the barns. Arriving at the construction site, we drove off the pavement onto the gravel bed for the new road where we were to spread our loads. The truck in front of me slowed, so I downshifted and slowed as well. Except, of course, that I had no idea how to stop an overloaded dump truck driving on wet gravel with wet brakes. The big olive drab hood of my truck began to crumple up before my eyes as I plowed into the back of the truck ahead.

The Lieutenant in charge came over, looked at the crumpled hood, broken grill, and fluids leaking onto the ground and said, "Can you drive it?" I said I thought so, and he directed me where to dump the load. Upon further examination, the truck was declared to be non-drivable, and a tow bar was procured. The tow bar was V-shaped, with the point of the V attached to the towing vehicle and the two arms attached to either side of the bumper of the disabled one. The arms were fastened by two steel pins and held in place by spring clips. We didn't have any clips, so we made some out of welding rod. The Lieutenant looked me in the eye and said, "It's now noon on Saturday. You have this truck on the line and ready to go Monday morning!" Yes, Sir!

I climbed into the cab of my truck, and the other driver got into his, and off we went. I was contemplating how I would fix this wreck when suddenly it was veering sharply to the right, headed for the ditch. I grabbed

Bigger Wheels

the steering wheel, turned sharply to the left, hit the brakes and the horn all at once. And once more, the truck in front stopped first. Bam! It seems the clips we had fashioned were substandard allowing one of the pins to slip out. We re-attached the tow bar. Undaunted and grateful that no one was injured, we completed the journey back to base.

Now I had no mechanical skills at all. My grandfather may have been a highly skilled master tool and die maker, but I was a klutz, a disgrace to my German forebears. Fortunately, the U.S. Army, recognizing this, provided a very detailed manual for every rifle, typewriter, shovel, and vehicle it owned. Complete with pictures. I grabbed the two-inch thick manual out of the map compartment and turned to the section on "How to disassemble one (each) truck, M52, 5-ton, dump." I spent the next day and a half with some very big wrenches taking the hood and grill off and the radiator out. Then used some very big hammers to beat the parts back into shape (except for the radiator, it was toast). I persuaded a mechanic to do a little welding on the broken parts, then I put it all back together. I grabbed a can of paint, olive drab, and slapped it on (hearing Dad in my head saying "Put some paint on it!"). Monday morning, I was ready to go. I lengthened my stopping distances and safely completed the rest of my sixty-day mission. (Well, except for the time that the truck caught fire in the middle of the munitions depot, but that wasn't really my fault. The fire went out, and I tightened a nut and drove out of there without blowing up the joint.)

Undeterred, I decided I wanted to drive even more, so I applied for a transfer to the 55th Transportation Company (55th TC) where guys were happily driving gasoline tankers all over the countryside. Freedom and paid sightseeing awaited me. Until I drove my jeep off the road in a rainstorm, hit a concrete guard post that was not hollow, and nearly got killed. My license was suspended. My transfer never came through.

Shortly after the jeep accident, I wrote a letter to my mother and described the accident. Then I wrote:

> "I don't want to tell you this to frighten you, but just to bring out a point. Most of the people who saw the jeep after the accident commented on how 'lucky' we were to get out alive, and with as minor injuries as we did. I feel that, again, God has intervened and saved my life as He did on that July 4th when I almost drowned, and on numerous other occasions. Each day I grow to appreciate life so much

more, and become more convinced that God has a definite purpose in mind for me. I hope and pray that I will find strength to do the tasks He has set before me."

God was not through with me yet.

> "Iron sharpens iron, and one
> man sharpens another."
> Proverbs 27:17 ESV

Chapter 10
A New Direction

My friend Mick Van Zandt introduced me to the Navigators, a Christian ministry for servicemen and college students. Navigator coordinators were posted worldwide, wherever the US military was stationed. They were tasked to organize retreats and programs and to train up servicemen to witness to their units. The purpose was to reach the lost and teach Christians to mature in their faith and ability to witness.

I had met Mick while standing in line at the base movie theater. The moment I saw him, I knew he was a Christian, and from then on we walked in faith like brothers, studying scripture, praying, and attending worship. We'd attend Navigator retreats

A New Direction

and events where I learned some of the disciplines that were lacking in my life such as Bible study and memorization, regular prayer, and increasing my trust in Jesus Christ. At these retreats I was encouraged by other guys who had the same struggles with temptations as I was having.

Our move to Sidi Brahim gave us a different chapel and a different Chaplain, Captain Kenneth Adcock, who was a Baptist. The combination of a good friend, Navigator training, and a caring godly Chaplain was a great help and encouragement to me. I became more confident in my faith and more open in my witness among the men I served with. Together, Mick and I would invite other guys to join us in study and worship.

Not that it was all serious. Mick had a quirky sense of humor that offset my far too serious approach to life. I bought a ukulele through mail order from a Sears catalog. I'd play silly songs and some Kingston Trio stuff I knew, and we'd sing and laugh in the evenings in the barracks. Mick and I are still friends today, more than fifty years later. He lives in Canada now, and we correspond at Christmas time each year, still sharing the faith and encouraging each other.

Tom Stickland was another story. He also had an oddball sense of humor and an independent spirit, and he loved to argue. Tom owned a powerful motorcycle, a 650cc BSA that was very fast and very loud. You could hear him coming a mile away. There were times at night in my bunk when I'd hear in the distance the sound of Tom returning to base, and I'd be grateful that he'd made it home safely.

I didn't drink when I entered the army. I had seen the damage that alcohol could do in the lives of my own family, especially in the life of my mother. So I had resisted the temptation to join in the drinking that goes on when young men gather. The first time I ever got drunk was with Tom at the base bowling alley. As we staggered back to the barracks, I asked him what to expect. He said the room would spin when I lay down and that I might get sick, but I'd be okay in the morning. I just fell asleep.

On New Year's Eve 1962, Tom and I went to a movie. When we returned to the barracks, I said I didn't want to be there when the drunks came back and started fighting and puking. So we persuaded the night duty driver to give us a ride to a small adjacent village where we found a cozy family tavern. There were several local families there and no other GIs. We ordered a bottle of red wine, a plate of French fries, and a cribbage board. We ate and drank and played cards while the people around us quietly celebrated the coming New Year. We ordered more wine

A New Direction

and fries, and when the clock struck midnight, everyone cheered. The tavern owner's daughter visited each table and gave everyone a commemorative key chain and a kiss. Tom and I left soon after and I suggested we not walk along the roadway lest we be struck down by some drunk driver. Instead, I said we should walk across the country using dead reckoning to get back to base. So we went, stumbling over frozen furrows in the farm fields, using our Army training to carefully traverse the barbed wire fences and amazingly arrived at the rear of the base in the early morning. The barracks were quiet except for the snoring, and we hit our bunks very happy to have welcomed 1963 in such a peaceful fashion.

Tom's tour of duty was up that summer, and he went back to Wisconsin, leaving me the proud owner of his motorcycle. I thought I'd never see Tom again, but God had a different plan.

Frankly, the motorcycle terrified me. As much as I loved freedom and speed, it was just too much. I quickly sold it and bought a used Vespa scooter. It was a fun ride, great in traffic, and cheap to run. Gas was about a dollar a gallon in France and Germany, while back in the States it was still less than a quarter. Unfortunately, the Vespa was not very reliable, which put me in more danger than the big motorcycle ever had.

There was a Navigator retreat over in Germany, and Mick and I decided to go. He would travel by train, but I decided it would be cheaper to ride the Vespa. It was fun for a while until I got on the Autobahn in Germany. There was no speed limit on the Autobahn—not for cars, not for trucks. The Vespa, on a good day, could manage sixty miles per hour. With cars going twice that fast, and trucks speeding by, I trudged along in the right lane. The Vespa decided not to have a good day. On uphill grades, it stalled out completely, and I had to get off and push it along the shoulder of the road. On downhill grades I'd jump back on, and it would run. Thankfully, I found my exit and began a long uphill trek to the lodge where the retreat was taking place. I finally decided I'd had enough. It was getting dark, and I still had a way to go, pushing that stupid Vespa. So I tossed the thing into a ditch and walked the rest of the way. Mick had been concerned because I missed the beginning of the retreat, but he was relieved when I walked into the room.

The retreat was, as usual, well run and a faith-filled time of learning and renewal. It was good to be with these men and to experience the blessing and strengthening of the Holy Spirit.

Over the next day or so, as I explained my plight, one of the men who had an Opel

A New Direction

station wagon offered to go with me to pick up the Vespa and take it to town for repairs. We found it still lying in the ditch and hoisted it out to put it in the car. It wouldn't fit. However, I had an idea, one of those "Here, hold my beer and watch this" moments (although I was completely sober). My friend produced a rope, one end of which we tied to his rear bumper and the other end of which we looped around the handlebar of the Vespa. He got in the car and I got on the Vespa, and we headed down the twisting, narrow mountain road. I did not have time to enjoy what I'm certain was the lovely scenery as we descended, because I was riding the brakes to keep from crashing into the Opel. We finally arrived at a repair shop, where I explained to the mechanic in fractured German that my Vespa would not go and that I'd be back the next day and would he fix it, please? "Ja," he said.

I picked up the supposedly repaired Vespa and headed for home. The trip back to base was even worse than the outbound journey had been. It involved another breakdown on the Autobahn, a ride in a German moving van, emergency bunking at a base in Karlsruhe, Germany, another attempt at repair, a third breakdown in an obscure German village, leaving the Vespa in the care of a bewildered gas station owner in said village, a ride in a German gasoline tanker to a train station where, ironically, I boarded a train to take me back to the base. Saved a lot of money on that trip.

I told a friend at the base where the Vespa was and said he could have it if he went to get it. A few weeks later, I went to Mick and said. "Give me seventy-five dollars, I just bought us a car." "What do we need a car for?" he asked. "Never mind, just trust me," I said.

In November of 1963, my thoughts were turning toward home. I stayed in touch with Mom, Dad, and Grandma Burtner with infrequent letters and even wrote to brother John and sister Joanne. I'd been in France for nearly two and a half years, isolated from all that was going on back in the States. One evening, most of us were in the village. There was a woman who set up her wagon in the village square where she served up french-fried potatoes (frites) and sausage sandwiches. The fries were wrapped in a cone of newspaper, and they were delicious. On this particular evening, word began coming out of the taverns—President Kennedy had been assassinated! Without any prompting or orders, all the GIs went back to the base. We all changed out of our civilian clothes and put on our combat uniforms. There was no official word. Was this an isolated incident, or were we about to go to war? No one knew. I got out my ukulele

A New Direction

and started singing some of the silly songs. A few guys criticized me, saying I should be more respectful. But I suggested it was important to keep our spirits up so we'd be ready for whatever was to come. The next day, we were called into formation and told what had happened. Although I'm certain that some of the combat units remained on high alert, we engineers went back to our routine tasks.

The car I bought over Mick's objections was a four-door Renault of uncertain vintage. It had a water-cooled rear engine, and it ran. A friend asked me for a ride to the air base one day, and I was happy to oblige. Wheels and freedom, that's all that mattered. On the way, I glanced in the rearview mirror and noticed flames coming out of the engine compartment. I calmly said to my friend, "I'm going to pull off onto the shoulder and stop the car. As soon as we're stopped, grab your gear, get out, and run that way," pointing out the windshield. We both ran, but as soon as the motor was stopped, the flames died. I got a tow to the air base and found a loose fuel line. I fixed it, and, except for a lingering burnt odor, the car was fine. Which was a good thing because it allowed us to go to Paris.

Two of our buddies were going home for Christmas and they asked if Mick and I would drive them. I think they even paid us.

So we packed up some cold fried chicken from the mess hall and set off early in the morning for Paris. About four hours later, we arrived at Orly airport and accompanied our friends into the terminal to see them off. Then we boarded a bus that would take us into that great city. The Champs-Elysees was all lit up for Christmas and a light snow was falling. It was magical. We walked and gaped and took a lot of pictures. Thanks to the United Service Organizations (USO), we found a clean, cheap hotel, the Hotel Dahlia's on Rue Des Acacias. We bought a bottle of wine and a loaf of bread and feasted in our room on bread, cold chicken, and wine. The next morning we rose and breakfasted on fresh bakery and strong coffee. Then we walked up that magnificent boulevard to the Arc de Triomphe and saw the eternal flame. Because my tour of duty was almost up, I had already shipped most of my personal civilian clothes home, which left me with sort of a ragtag outfit. Mick took a picture of me looking cold and a little lost there at the base of the arch.

On New Year's Eve 1963 Mick and I spent some time together. The last week on post had been busy. We had gone to visit a friend who was in jail and prayed with him. Clearing base, turning in my gear, and saying goodbye to my buddies was a little like leaving home after thirty-one months.

A New Direction

One of those goodbyes as I boarded the bus the next day has stuck in my mind. The guy's name was Whiteman. He was a smart guy and quite the cynic. He'd always given me a hard time about the Christian faith and enjoyed mocking me. He thought that faith in Christ was foolish. Once I had said to him, "If I'm wrong about Christ, then I will have been a fool for a few years on Earth. If you're wrong, you will suffer for it for all eternity." That day, just before I boarded the bus, Whiteman came and shook my hand and said, "Keep the faith." Perhaps a seed had been planted.

The bus took us to Metz, and a train brought me again to Bremerhaven where I was among the last to board the aging troopship, the USNS Geiger, that would take me home and through yet one more dangerous adventure.

The North Atlantic in the winter is not a happy place; its reputation for deadly storms is well earned. Because I was one of the last to board the ship, all duty assignments for the voyage had already been made. So basically I spent the time hiding out with a small group of similarly-situated individuals in a corridor adjacent to the galley (kitchen). The guys who worked in the galley had to cross our corridor to serve the officer's mess (dining room). Since we were all brothers-in-arms, the galley crew would bring us food, sandwiches, fruit, and cake. So we sat and talked, some reading scripture or novels, some playing cards, idling our time away. Until the pipes started breaking and water flooded the corridor.

It was a huge storm lasting more than two days. They battened down all the hatches, closed the watertight doors, and trapped us inside. Looking out of a porthole, the waves were so high you could not see the sky. The next moment the ship would be perched on top of a wave and you could not see the water. At night in our racks down below, we could feel the whole ship vibrate as the propeller came up out of the sea and beat the air. Water began to slosh up and down the corridors as pipes broke and hatches leaked. It was terrifying.

After the storm subsided and the hatches were opened, we were still riding the giant swells of the ocean. Debris was scattered all over the deck, life rafts had broken loose and washed overboard. We breathed in the cold salt air thankfully and looked toward home. We were a little late getting there.

The skyline of New York City came into view early on Sunday morning, January 12, 1964. As glad as I was to be home, soon to walk on solid ground again, I began to feel depressed. Because it was Sunday, I was certain we'd have to spend one more night

A New Direction

in the Army, sleeping in some cramped barracks until Monday came. I was wrong.

Our battered ship, bound for a major overhaul we heard, docked at Brooklyn Navy Yard. They marched us to the processing center, and I began my long-awaited separation from active duty. There was a form to sign stating I had no lingering health issues. Eager to get out, I ignored the back pain that resulted from my jeep accident and checked the box that said "None." Next we stood in line to get paid: final monthly pay (prorated), unpaid leave, and anything else we were due. I received one hundred thirty-five dollars and change. The last line I ever stood in as a soldier in the US Army was the travel pay line. Guys in front of me were getting plane tickets to Los Angeles, train tickets to Pittsburg, and bus tickets to New Jersey. When I stepped up to the window, they handed me a subway token. Clad in my class A uniform and lugging my duffle bag, I trudged out into the street in search of the nearest subway station. I was home.

That evening, after supper at my grandparents' house, we gathered in the living room to watch The Ed Sullivan Show on television. That's when it hit me. 'What did they do to my country while I was away?"

"For here we have no lasting city, but we seek the city that is to come."
Hebrews 13:14 ESV

Chapter 11

ANOTHER COUNTRY

The next day I celebrated my twenty-first birthday, but with a growing feeling of discontent. Everything had changed since 1961. There was a looseness, a sense of rebellion, in the air. Attitudes were different; there was open mocking of established values, and everything seemed to be tinged with a smirk. The television commercials offended me, loud and brash and talking down to me. I had grown both in faith and in character during my three-year stint in the Army, but none of that seemed sufficient to confront this new world.

I thought I could pick up my life again, a little stronger than before, a little less vulnerable to my past and my family dramas.

Another Country

I went back to the First Reformed Church, got involved with the youth group as sort of a member emeritus, and got reacquainted with old friends. But the changes were too much. I'd hear comments such as, "Oh, I know your father" or "I'm friends with your cousin" and began to realize that in this town I had a ghost family, one I'd never known.

I went to New Jersey. Mom and Ed had bought a house in the Pompton Lakes area. I got off the bus in town and was greeted by my sister Joanne, now twelve years old. I met my newest sister, Helen, almost three years old, who had been born while I was in basic training. And when I walked into the house, I saw John, my little brother, now fifteen years old. While I was away he had grown from a short little league baseball player into a six foot, three-inch basketball terror. My first impulse was to apologize for any wrongs I might have done him as a child, and I especially hoped he wouldn't hold against me that time I tried to hang him. Fortunately, John was gracious and forgiving. It was good to see them all. I took Helen to town and bought her a doll.

Mom looked tired, and I could tell she had still not found the happiness she so desperately wanted. It was evident that she was drinking more. Ed hadn't changed. He was still the smug, overconfident, domineering, egotistical master of the house he'd always been. Although we were able to be cordial with each other, it took me a long time to forgive him. Eventually, I did, if only because I realized that it took two to wreck a home.

Later that January, I made a trip to the Navigator headquarters in Colorado Springs. I spent a week there in the beautiful snow-covered foothills of the Rockies. I worked in the print shop and met many wonderful servants of God. But I never felt called to join them, so I went home to New York and tried to find a job.

The lumber company that hired me did so on the recommendation of Ed's son, Ed III. He was still a contractor and a good customer of Kahn's Lumber and Millwork in Flushing. I drove delivery trucks for them, but I was not fast enough or good enough, and my tenure with them was brief.

My friend Bob Zittel was dating Barbara Maier, a cute girl with a charming German tinge to her Queens accent. Her father was vice-president of Traulsen, Inc., a local manufacturer of premium commercial refrigerators. He liked me, so I was in. I started on the factory floor, which was a study in cultural dynamics. Many of the workers were Puerto Rican immigrants, the first generation to move en masse to New York. Most of the supervisors and executives were first generation Germans, Mr. Maier himself having been an officer in the German Luftwaffe. The cultural gulf was immense. Yet surprisingly, everything ran smoothly, and the team turned out first class quality products.

Mr. Maier had visions of me learning the business and eventually moving into marketing and sales. Me, I just wanted a job. I eventually drifted toward the shipping department and began driving one of the two delivery trucks. Which is how I got my education in the dark side: union corruption.

I was, of course, a union member; you had to be to work anywhere. The refrigerators I delivered ranged in size from single units about the same size as the ones in the average home to double and triple units that could weigh over a thousand pounds. The first incident occurred at a major hospital renovation project in Manhattan. When I arrived, the site union rep told me to hold up on the dock. He disappeared and then returned with four other men, two electricians, a pipefitter, and a refrigeration guy. They had clocked out of whatever they were doing and were now clocked in as helping to handle the refrigerator. Except, of course, they didn't help. They stood on the dock, watching as I struggled to unload the oversized ice box off the truck. When I none-too-meekly suggested they earn their pay by actually participating in the unloading, all four took offense. So I left the thing on the dock, and they returned to their work. Or not.

Traulsen also made special refrigerators for ships which we exported. One day I had two such units to deliver to the docks. They weren't large, but were fully crated. I drove to the dockyard and followed the long line of trucks through the gate. A forklift was unloading cargo from each truck, so I just parked in line, untied the crates and moved them to the tailgate. Nothing happened. Truck after truck was unloaded and left, only to be replaced by another truck which was unloaded. At first I thought maybe there was some priority for different types of cargo, or scheduling issues, but as the hours slipped away I began to get frustrated. Then a friendly driver came over. I asked why I wasn't being unloaded. He said, "Oh, you have to go see the yard steward." He pointed the way to a grubby little hole-in-the-wall office where I found a big, fat guy ensconced in a worn out swivel chair behind a cluttered desk. "Whatcha got?" he asked. I told him I had two refrigerators from Traulsen. "Ten bucks." he said. I gave him the ten out of my wallet, and my truck was the very next one unloaded. I was furious. When I got back to the factory, I explained to my boss that I was late because I had failed to pay a bribe immediately upon arriving at the dockyard. He just laughed and said in the future I should get the money from the office before going to the dockyard. Just a routine part of doing business in the Big Apple.

Bob, Barbara, and I became good friends. I started dating Sue Johnson, the daughter of my favorite Sunday School teacher Grace Johnson. Sue and I went to see the Beatles movie *A Hard Day's Night* and watched their American television debut on The Ed Sullivan Show. We attended dances, parties, and beach outings together, and it was all carefree fun.

I moved out of my grandparents' house and into a roach-infested apartment in a run-down, six-family building. Some friends from church donated the furnishings I needed, and I was content enough to be on my own. My army buddy Mick came to visit when his tour was over, before he went home to Washington. I gave him the grand tour of New York, including a trip upstate to see my grandfathers' old place in Sullivan County. We drove right up to the door of the house, and I asked permission to walk around and see the place. Mick was impressed, since his idea of New York was that it all looked like Manhattan.

Someone gave me a tip about a room for rent in a private home. It was a third floor single room with a private bath in a very clean and beautiful older home on the corner opposite the Poppenhusen monument, a College Point landmark.

During that first year home, I had started drinking again. I broke up with Sue. She deserved a younger boyfriend who would be more fun than a morose twenty-one-year-old who had no idea where he was going.

That same year my friend Lou Jones died as a result of a fire that occurred right around the corner from the roach-filled apartment where I lived. He had taught me to appreciate, if not love, culture, language, and classical music. He was disappointed when I, as a teenager, bought a guitar and wanted to play like the Everly Brothers, not Segovia. "You're going to strum, not pluck?" he exclaimed in dismay. He was fascinated by electronics and owned one of the first reel-to-reel tape recorders. It was this device that permitted me to hear my voice and caused me to hate my New York accent. Lou helped me understand why I sounded that way and when I asked for help, counseled me on how to change my speech. I worked hard at it, so that by the time I went to college in Iowa, they could not determine where I was from by listening. After his death, I wrote this in the front of the Bible he had given me:

> "Those whose signatures appear on the next two pages were responsible for making Christ real for me for the

first time, when I accepted Him as my Savior on August 31, 1957."

"And God bless the memory of Lou Jones, who taught me much about life and living, and who died too soon in 1964. He gave me this book and a little bit of himself. May he be at peace, with music and wine and conversation with his Lord."

"Where shall I go from your Spirit? Or where shall I flee from your presence? If I ascend to heaven, you are there! If I make my bed in Sheol, you are there! If I take the wings of the morning and dwell in the uttermost parts of the sea, even there your hand shall lead me, and your right hand shall hold me. If I say, "Surely the darkness shall cover me, and the light about me be night," even the darkness is not dark to you; the night is bright as the day, for darkness is as light with you."
Psalm 139:7-12 ESV

Chapter 12

THE PAST CATCHES UP

I was in my room one evening in 1965 when my landlady called on the house phone. "You have a visitor," she said. I went downstairs to the front door, and there stood a man I didn't know. He stuck out his hand and said, "Hi, Bob! I'm your dad."

When I was sixteen, I had a chance to get a summer job working in a drug store. Before I could work though, I had to get a work

The Past Catches Up

permit and a social security number, and for that I needed a birth certificate. When I approached the window at the County Clerk's office, I asked for a copy of my birth certificate. The clerk asked for my name and went to look through the files. She returned and said she couldn't find any birth records for Robert William Frohlich. Flustered, I left the building and found a phone booth and called home. "Mom," I asked, "what was my name when I was born?" She just sighed and told me. When I returned to the clerk's window, I asked for the birth records for Robert William Kaufman Jr. She came up with the file right away and cheerfully asked, "What name do you want on the copy?" "Frohlich," I said. After all, that was who I was.

Except now here stood Robert William Kaufman the senior. I was twenty-two years old, and this was the first time I'd ever seen the man. I invited him up. He started to talk, said he wanted to answer any questions I had. Questions! My mind was full of questions, not one of which could I articulate. Where were you all this time? Why did you leave? And what could you possibly want from me now? I was speechless.

He said he'd just retired from the Navy. He was married, had some kids and was planning to travel about the country in a camper. Would I like to come along, he asked.

"Come along?" screamed my mind. "I don't even know you. I don't want to know you!" But I just nodded. He said, "Did you know that your grandmother lives right around the corner from here?" That's what did it. It broke me inside. Here was a whole secret world I knew nothing about. Everywhere I went, I would keep on bumping into people who knew all about me. I had to get out. He left, promising to keep in touch. I can't remember anything else he said. I drank some whiskey and smashed my ukulele to bits.

Bob and Barbara were married, and I was the best man, a misnomer if there ever was one. During my drunken best man toast at the reception, I suggested that Bob was really the best man since he, not I, got the girl. After offending the maid of honor, I went to the men's room, puked, and lay there on the floor. Bob and Donald Plitt came to get me, begging me not to drive. I threw my car keys at them, and they drove me home. It was really time to go.

In the days that followed, I apologized to the maid of honor and took her to a movie and behaved myself. I'm sure I must have apologized to Bob and Barbara and everyone else I'd offended. I gave notice at work and to my landlady. About two weeks later, in early March, I loaded up my 1959 Rambler American with all my clothes, my

The Past Catches Up

typewriter, and a World War II bayonet that had been given to me for protection by a friend. I clipped it under the dashboard.

My grandparents were distraught. "What about your praying?" Grandma asked, using the German word for prayer. That's over, I thought. "Where are you going?" "Arizona," I said. I had three hundred dollars in my pocket and still owed about that much on the car. I was determined to get to Arizona, look up an old army buddy named Chilson, who once told me that if I ever needed a job, I should come out and drive dump trucks for his Dad. Of course, I never made it that far.

With a full tank of gas, everything I owned in the car, and a map, I headed west. The first part of the journey was familiar, retracing the route back toward Iowa. It was a relief to leave New York behind for good. Let the family work out their own troubles. I couldn't fix them. Why I thought I should be able to fix them was a question that did not occur to me. I didn't have a college degree. I was not on my way to becoming the next Billy Graham. I had mistreated my friends and disappointed everyone who cared for me. I had no plans, no dreams, no driving motivation except to escape. Surely God was through with me now. I just wanted to get out west and if I died in the desert, that would be just fine with me.

"I shall not die, but I shall live, and
recount the deeds of the Lord."
Psalm 118:17 ESV

Chapter 13

MY PLAN, GOD'S PLAN

I heard a noise, a faint but distinct clicking sound from underneath the car as I accelerated out of the toll booth in Indiana. (Really, what WAS it about me and Indiana?) I had driven all night from New York to New Jersey, across the Pennsylvania Turnpike, into Ohio, and through most of Indiana. It was early Sunday morning as I passed through the last toll booth in Indiana. The clicking noise grew more rapid as I picked up speed. Now, approaching Chicago I began to worry. If the car broke down here, in this city, on a Sunday, then by Monday I'd be broke too, after paying for towing, lodging and repairs. Chicago just sat there, unmoved, waiting to take my last three

My Plan, God's Plan

hundred dollars and suck me into its grasp. Perhaps I prayed. Pulling off the highway, I consulted a map. Where could I go? Then I noticed Racine, Wisconsin, just north of Chicago on the map. Tom Stickland lived in Racine. We hadn't corresponded since he left France, but he might still be there. I eased back out onto the highway heading north, being very gentle with my Rambler, hoping to leave Chicago behind to find help in Wisconsin.

The big rustic sign at the border welcomed me to Wisconsin. The air was so fresh, the sky so big and blue. There were trees and farm fields along the highway. As I neared Racine, I pulled off the highway and located a phone booth. Scanning the directory, I found the name "Stickland" and dialed the number. A woman answered, and I asked for Tom. She told me she was his mother, but that Tom didn't live there anymore. My heart sank. Then she said that Tom was living with a friend and gave me his number. Nervously, I dialed again and Tom answered the phone. "Hi Tom! It's Bob Frohlich, you know, from the Army." He remembered. I told him where I was and how my car was having problems and how I hoped he could help me get it fixed. Tom gave me directions to a shopping center near where he lived and told me he'd meet me there. I got back in the Rambler and gingerly continued north to the Racine exit at Highway 11, then turned east toward Racine.

Mrs. June Freimann, the mother of Tom's friend Donny, fed me more than once, as did Tom's parents, Mason and Joan Stickland. They gave me a place to sleep for a few nights. Tom took me to his favorite garage where they replaced the worn out universal joint in my Rambler for about fifteen dollars. I took a room at a hotel downtown and started to get reacquainted with Tom over beers at his favorite bar in Kenosha. Racine was a friendly enough place— not slap-you-on-the-back friendly, but mostly kind and helpful. It was a manufacturing city, home to S. C. Johnson of Johnson Wax fame, J. I. Case tractors, Jacobson Lawn equipment and dozens of other companies. There seemed to be a neighborhood tavern on every other corner, easily outnumbering the churches, which were plentiful and diverse in denomination. I went to the bars but didn't attend any of the churches.

It was March, and I was running low on cash. Tom and his fiancée, Sue Sorenson, were getting married in August, and Tom suggested I stick around until then. Sure, why not? I thought. I began to fill out job applications at all the major factories but wasn't having any luck getting hired. Tom said, "Why don't you try Moxness Products? They'll hire anybody." He was right. And if

My Plan, God's Plan

coming to Racine was a profound miracle of redirection straight from the hand of God, then getting a job a Moxness Products was an equally unexpected and profoundly life-changing event. Marleen Sheeder worked there.

I worked in the mill room weighing out the raw ingredients for making various silicone rubber compounds which were to be molded into various custom products. I would put the raw materials into the blending mill consisting of two smooth counter-rotating drums that applied heat and pressure to combine the ingredients into a moldable raw material for the extruders. As the drums rotated, I'd cut the material off the rollers with a sharp linoleum knife, and feed it back into the rollers until it was thoroughly blended. It was a little dangerous. To get your hand caught in the rollers meant crushed limbs. So I was very careful about where I put my hand. Unfortunately, I wasn't as careful with the sharp knife, so one day I cut a slice off the tip of my left thumb. Now, for a crushed hand they'd have called an ambulance, but for a bleeding thumb I got sent to the office, where they pointed out the typist who kept the first aid kit. The typist who dabbed my thumb with something and put an adhesive bandage on it stole my heart.

Marleen was a petite brown-haired, brown eyed girl with a small mouth and a sweet shy smile. Our first date was a cheap one. Tom got us tickets for a company picnic at Muskego Beach Park. We had a great time, playing carnival games, eating, walking, and talking. At one point, as we walked along, Marleen took my hand. I can still feel the electric shock of that first touch. I couldn't believe it. She likes me!

I lived in a rooming house on Main Street, and when I had time I would eat at George Webb on Main Street. Breakfast was fifty-two cents. But I didn't always eat. Marleen would bring a piece of toast from home sprinkled with sugar and cinnamon for me. There were more dates, more time getting to know one another.

Marleen was the middle child of seven, with three brothers and three sisters. Her father was also one of seven children, while her mother had two siblings. They were from Iowa, a small town called Adair, about 60 miles west of Des Moines. Marleen and her sister Darleen in 1961 went to work for Allied Mutual, an insurance company in Des Moines. That's how it came to be that we had Babe's Pizza in common. After her parents and younger siblings moved to Racine, Marleen and Darleen moved there in 1964 to rejoin them.

My Plan, God's Plan

Marleen had grown up on a farm, learning to do chores very early in life. In the early grades she attended a one-room school heated by a wood stove. She learned to cook and bake with her grandmother, preparing big meals for the hired help on her grandfather's farm. The Sheeder family did not attend church except for a few occasions during Marleen's life on the farm.

The Rambler had suffered much abuse during my pre-Marleen late night trips home from the bars, so I decided what I really needed was a new car. I went to every new car dealer in town with the same pitch: "I want a new, two-door, six-cylinder car with manual transmission, preferably blue. I have only this Rambler for a down payment. If you can get me financed, we've got a deal." The Ford, Chevy and Rambler dealers all fell short. But at the Plymouth dealer, I hit pay dirt. "I've got just what you want," said the salesman as he led me to the back lot. It was a brand new 1965 Plymouth Valiant, two-door, six-cylinder, stick shift in Blue Metallic. Financing was obtained, and the car was mine. Vinyl seats, rubber floor, no carpet. But it was mine! It even had a radio. Immediately, I took it to Tom's favorite garage, cut out the factory muffler and installed a mellow sounding glass pack replacement. It was mine.

Marleen thought I was rich, new car and all. We were in love, and it did not matter what she thought. Then I almost blew it.

Marleen went away for a few days, flying south to Memphis to visit some old friends. When she returned, some little thing she said, or maybe the way she said it turned me off. I stopped calling. Naturally, I was miserable. After a few weeks I was moping around, complaining to Tom that I didn't have anything to do that weekend. He said, "Why don't you call Marleen?" Now Marleen had a habit of saying "I don't care," whenever I asked about where we should go or what we should do. It was just an expression, but I didn't like it. So I made up my mind to call her and ask her to a movie. If she said, "I don't care," I would hang up and that would be the end of it. So I called. "Hi, this is Bob. Would you like to go to a movie?" "I'd love to," she replied. God is good, even to fools like me.

On December 11th, 1965, Marleen and I were going to attend a company Christmas party with Tom and Sue. I was selling used cars by then, and I borrowed a beautiful white 1964 Plymouth Fury with a red interior. Marleen had bought a special dress and even had shoes dyed to match. I picked her up at home and after we got in the car, I pulled a ring out of my pocket, offered it to her and said, "I want you to be my wife." She

My Plan, God's Plan

didn't say a word, but accepted the ring and we kissed. "Do you want to go back inside and tell your folks?" I asked. "No, let's just go," she said, smiling.

We drove over to Tom and Sue's apartment to pick them up. Marleen left her dyed shoes in the car, and we went in. When we came back to the car, her shoes were gone. She had to wear her regular black high heels that night, but I didn't care. It was a great party, a great evening, and we were glowing in anticipation of a new life together.

Now there were decisions to make. When should we get married? Soon, we decided. Where should we get married? We needed to find a church. Marleen said that there had been a Methodist Church in her home town, and she'd been there once or twice. So we began to attend Bethany Methodist Church and planned our wedding for Saturday, April 9, 1966. But first I thought it would be proper for Marleen to meet my family. We flew out to New York and stayed with my grandparents. Marleen met the whole clan. It was all very cordial of course, and everyone thought Marleen was wonderful, and that I was a very lucky man. I agreed, except I would have used the word "blessed." Marleen had one request though. After seeing New York City, she said on the way home, "Promise me we'll never move here."

That was a promise I was glad to make and eager to keep.

Marleen's mom and dad were taciturn, hardworking people. Her dad worked for a tree service, planting and trimming trees and shrubs. Her mom worked in a factory. She was a quiet, pleasant woman, who could cook up big meal for the family and guests. Marleen's dad was building an attached garage and carport out of used building materials he had hauled home in his pickup truck. Four of Marleen's siblings still lived at home: Darleen, Linda, Virgil, and Twila, the youngest. Darleen was dating Dave Christensen at the time, so we'd have a full crew hammering away at the construction project. I was introduced to Iowa farm cuisine, which included lots of sweet corn.

Marleen's family was immense. We traveled back to Adair to meet the brothers, Larry and Orville, their wives, Donna and Janice, and their children. There were also two sets of grandparents and endless streams of aunts, uncles, and cousins. It was impossible to keep them all straight in my mind.

Our wedding day arrived, and Tom, my best man, drove me to the church. It snowed lightly that day. When we got to the church, I asked Tom to drive around the block one more time. I was nervous. As the ceremony was about to begin, I took my place up front,

My Plan, God's Plan

and the music started. I panicked when Marleen did not come into view right away. But then she did, a petite slender vision in a beautiful white dress. We said all the words, exchanged rings and then we were man and wife. Our reception was in the church basement—cake and coffee only. Tom's brother, Gerald, took the wedding photos in black and white. My Dad, Bill, was there. Then it was time to go. Tom drove us back to our apartment to change, with Marleen's family in hot pursuit in a variation of a chiveree.

We changed, packed, and drove to Elkhorn, Wisconsin for our weekend honeymoon. Our car was a 1953 Plymouth, because I'd sold my new car after I became a car salesman. For one thing, I didn't need a car because I could always drive a demonstrator. Secondly, I was such a terrible car salesman that I couldn't afford the payments. I'd also persuaded Marleen to sell her car, a nice 1963 Ford because I felt we couldn't afford those payments either. So, a 1953 Plymouth it was. We spent two nights in the "honeymoon suite" at Sterlingworth Motor Lodge. On Sunday, upon recommendation of the motel staff, we went to the White Horse Inn just down the road on Highway 12. We enjoyed the house special, a sirloin for two and a nice bottle of wine. For many years we returned to the White Horse Inn for our anniversary dinner.

On Monday, we took care of business at home, buying life insurance and furniture and getting everything set up. Marleen brought into the marriage a very nice bedroom suite and a black and white television. The rest we bought at the furniture store across the street. Our apartment was one of six above a hardware store. It had a living room, bedroom, kitchen, and bath. It was about five blocks from Moxness, where Marleen still worked, and about a mile to the Varsity Boot Shop, a family shoe store where I now worked. Marleen was earning sixty-five dollars a week as a clerk typist and I started out at sixty dollars a week at the shoe store. Rent was seventy dollars a month, and for twenty dollars we could buy all the groceries we needed at the A&P store across the parking lot from our apartment. Thus, about thirteen months after arriving in Racine with a broken car, less than three hundred dollars, and only one friend, I was now married, employed, and settled. I could not believe it.

I never did make it to Arizona. Years later, whenever someone asked how a New Yorker like me came to settle in Racine I'd say, "This is where my car broke down."

"The one who offers thanksgiving as his sacrifice glorifies me; to one who orders his way rightly I will show the salvation of God!"
Psalm 50:23 ESV

Chapter 14

A NEW LIFE

Early on in our marriage, I tried to talk with Marleen about faith. She had no context for that discussion, and I was a less than perfect specimen of Christian manhood. But I tried, and over the years, after attending church together, she began to understand. Then, by her own efforts to study and know the Bible, and by the Grace of God, Marleen came to faith and received the gift of new life in Christ. God's Grace was and is the main reason our marriage has endured.

Marleen's mother, Helen, became quite ill right after our wedding, and in September 1966 she died. Marleen cried out, "Now she'll never see my babies!" It was a hard time, and I did not have the words to comfort her. So I just held her as she cried. Now her Dad, Kenneth, was left to raise a nine-year-old daughter, Twila, on his own.

The following year I began to grow restless. We wanted to start a family, but the shoe store wasn't going to provide the income we'd need. When we first dated, Marleen said she wanted a dozen children. I was hoping to talk her down some. I went to the employment office seeking help. They administered intelligence and aptitude tests and cheerfully informed me that, with the right education, I could be anything: doctor, lawyer, engineer. I said going to college was not an option; I had responsibilities now. So their advice to me was to get an entry level job at a large company and work my way up.

After submitting many applications, I received two job offers in one day. One was for a factory sweeper job at about $2.60 per hour and the other was a laborer job at Wisconsin Natural Gas Company starting at $2.35 per hour. As Marleen and I discussed these opportunities, I thought the gas company job was probably less likely to have cyclical layoffs and would therefore be more secure. Since my only goal had been to land a job that paid more than two bucks an hour, the gas company was the right choice.

A New Life

And once again, it was more providential than I ever could imagine.

The men I worked with starting in mid-September 1967 were careful and hardworking. We installed new gas mains and services in residential areas. We were also called on to make repairs on older pipe in the ground. Our crew consisted of a crew leader, an excavator operator, a welder, a distribution man who assembled the pieces and parts, and me, a laborer who did whatever else needed doing. I learned quickly and enjoyed the outdoors, the company of the men, and the feeling of accomplishment at the end of the day. I joined the union and was pleasantly surprised by the tenor of the meetings and the mostly thoughtful discussions. These men worked hard and negotiated in good faith. I'd attend the monthly meetings and go to the bars afterwards. I joined the company bowling league.

By the first of the year in 1968, Marleen and I were debt free and enjoying our life together. There was a pizza place a block away, so we'd treat ourselves to pizza about once a week. We socialized with Tom and Sue and with Tom's brother Gerald and his wife Dorie.

We drove back to New York once, enjoying a happy visit with Bob and Barbara and their firstborn child. Less happy was our visit with Mom and Ed. She was sad and drinking, and I just walked out. Later that day I phoned her and rebuked her when she said she was happy and that Ed loved her. I said she was obviously not happy and that Ed was just using her and making her life miserable. After I hung up, I turned to Marleen and said, "I just said goodbye to my mom." I thought it was for the last time.

Eager to start our family, we moved into an upper flat on Gilson Street in a nice neighborhood. It had two bedrooms, a living room, bath, and kitchen. We had access to a laundry area in the basement and half of the two car garage. There was a small backyard with a huge silver maple tree. The downstairs neighbors, the Rasmussens, were young like us. Jim, a policeman, and his wife, Charley, became good friends. In the ensuing years we socialized, dined and camped with them. At one time we were members of the same church.

I got the springtime urge again, and we bought our first new car, a 1968 Volkswagen in powder blue. It cost two thousand four dollars, tax included, and it was a fun-to-drive, reliable car that Marleen actually liked. Marleen was pregnant by now and on November 22, 1968 our daughter, Robin, was born.

It was a Thursday night, and I was out bowling with my team. Marleen wasn't due for a few weeks yet, but when I got home

A New Life

around half past nine, her water broke. We grabbed her things and jumped in the car, headed for St. Luke's hospital. In just a couple of hours, at 2:55 AM, it was over, and we were parents. "That was the easiest thing I've ever done!" said my beaming wife. Looking down on that sweet child, I couldn't believe this wonderful new life was given to us.

Now, in addition to my spoken wedding vows which I meant with all my heart, I made personal vows that I would not, ever, make a mess of things the way my parents had done. I would never lie, never cheat, never abuse my wife or my children. Nothing would ever be more important in my life than my family. They were to be my number one priority. Forever. Given my less than auspicious beginnings, that was a lot of pressure. And not putting God first was a serious mistake.

But I was a dad now, cheerfully changing diapers and getting up at night to prepare Robin for feeding before Marleen would nurse her. We held her, bathed her, dressed her, played with her, and had her baptized at Providence Church of Christ.

About that time, a job opening was posted for a serviceman fitter. I had begun a home study course on the basics of the natural gas industry, so I was well-prepared to take the necessary exam to get the job. After acing the test, I started work in the service department at the bottom of the nine-step pay scale for servicemen. And I had a goal: to become the best serviceman in the department and to get to the top of that pay scale as quickly as possible. The guys who trained me on the job were mostly patient, and a few were very skilled. I learned the basic routines and gradually began to perform the furnace and appliance repairs we offered. We also investigated gas odor reports, tracked down leaks, made repairs, and called in crews when the leaks were underground. With overtime pay and night callouts, I was making good money, but I also learned to love the utility business of providing safe and reliable service to our customers who depended on us. Sounds like a slogan, but I really believed it. I got to meet customers from all different income levels, races, and ages and found it to be fascinating. We also served many small business owners. Everything was an education in human relations.

I loved the job. Sometimes we'd go out in teams of two to do piping jobs. It was fun when I'd get with another guy who really liked to work—we'd bang out a really productive day. One day I was partnered with Harry Hansen, a guy about my age. We were sent to a certain neighborhood to do inside meter rebuilds. The job consisted of shutting off

A New Life

the gas, disassembling the meter piping and then rebuilding the whole thing according to a new, safer standard. Most crews did two or three a day, maybe four on a really good day. Harry and I quickly figured a standard approach and hit it hard. We ate our lunches quickly in the truck then kept on. We did seven rebuilds. In union terms, we killed the job. When I handed in our paperwork to the boss, I tried to soft-pedal the whole thing, saying we'd been lucky, they were all easy. But he knew and we knew and it was a great day.

I bought a used 1961 GMC pickup to drive to work so that Marleen could have the car during the day. She was going to be a stay-at-home mom since family was her number one priority too.

My grandparents came for a visit to see their first great-grandchild. Grandma was delighted because we looked "so prosperous" with two cars and all. Later that year, Mom came with Ed to see her granddaughter. But Robin was going through a stage where she cried when strangers were around, so Mom was thwarted in her one chance to bond with her first grandchild. She spoke often of this disappointment in later years

On Sundays, we went to the Providence church. Marleen was baptized and became a member. We were as active in the life of the congregation as a young couple with a small child could be.

In 1969, we bought a house. We both wanted to be out of town a little, in a place where we could have a garden and another child. The place we bought was just west of the city on Spring Street. It was a small and not-very-well-built two-bedroom house, eight hundred thirty-two square feet on two and a half acres. The lot was one hundred feet wide and eleven hundred feet deep. Plenty of room for a garden or an airstrip.

Using heretofore undiscovered skills, I laid new sub-flooring, tiled the kitchen, rebuilt the plumbing, installed a new gas furnace to replace the old oil-fired one, and built a fence and a shed. Not all at once of course. I insulated the attic, installed gutters and downspouts, tilled up a garden where we grew corn, green beans, peas, carrots, potatoes and more, and built a sandbox, a dog house, and a play kitchen. I felt like a homesteader.

Our daughter Starr was born June 20, 1972 at 11:22 PM, I was home this time, but it was a great surprise because she arrived almost five weeks early. We bundled up Robin and dropped her off at Grandpa Sheeder's house, then raced to the hospital. It was quick. Starr was impatient and it was over in no time. Another beautiful healthy girl and again a beaming wife.

A New Life

We were happy in our little house. Marleen was born to be a mom, and she thrived at it. We were now members of Franksville United Methodist Church, where Starr was baptized. We were still looking for a congregation where we both felt comfortable. And there was another big change, I finally quit smoking for good.

In 1971, we had made another trip out east to visit family and friends in New York and my brother in Nova Scotia. John was now married and working there after attending Acadia University. We were driving in our big 1968 Chrysler Newport, Marleen and I in the front bench seat with Robin sitting between us. As we were driving though New England, Robin started a pantomime that shook me. She reached out and touched the cigarette lighter, then paused for a few seconds. Then she reached out again, pretending to take the lighter out of its socket, and with her other hand pretended to put a cigarette in her mouth which she pretended to light with a satisfied puff. Then she replaced the lighter in its socket. I was appalled. She was not even three years old at the time. What was I teaching her?

So in 1972, while Marleen and Starr were still in the hospital, I sat on our bed at home and asked God to help me quit, right then, so that Starr would never see me smoke. She never did. God gave me the strength to say "I'm not smoking today" whenever I was offered a cigarette. It gradually got easier until I could honestly say "I don't smoke." That was the first gift big sister Robin gave little sister Starr.

Robin was blond haired, blue eyed, and very content to amuse herself. She was happy, curious, quiet, and very neat. Starr had beautiful brown hair and blue eyes. She was very active and curious, always wanting to take charge of her environment and independent to a fault. They were a joy. They even got along well together most of the time. Each one had a lovely voice, and they'd sing together sometimes. Once, when they were both adults, I sang with them before the congregation at the Franksville church. The song was recorded, and it is one of my most precious memories.

"For I know the plans I have for you, declares the Lord, plans for welfare and not for evil, to give you a future and a hope."
Jeremiah 29:11 ESV

Chapter 15

MOVING UP

One day at work in 1973, I was called to the personnel office and asked to consider applying for a new position that was being created—gas control specialist. The job was to be staffed by four individuals working rotating shifts to cover twenty-four hours every day, seven days a week. The task was to monitor system load to ensure adequate supply and pressures for our customers and to stay within contract parameters with our pipeline supplier. Working with a dispatcher, we also did off-hours emergency work dispatching. There were about twenty applicants for the job already, but personnel wanted me to apply as well. I said, "Why not?"

I went home that day and informed Marleen that I'd just applied for a really crappy job. She said, "If it's so crappy, why did you apply for it?" I explained that this job touched every part of the company; its suppliers, its delivery system, and its operating personnel. I'd be exposed to people in engineering, distribution, accounting, and customer service—people at all levels of management. I'd learn more about the company than most other employees. They tested me, of course, and I was notified shortly that I was one of the four chosen.

Now the really great thing about an entirely new position is that the people who created it thought they knew what the job was, but it was the people in the job who molded it into what it needed to be. And we were a smart and gutsy group, Barry, Jim, Joy, and me. With differing backgrounds in the company, we fed off each other. We were not rivals; we were co-conspirators, determined to make this work. We invented procedures, created new forms, and endlessly tweaked to make things work better. It was great fun, and it was awful.

The great fun was creating the job. We had a boss, Harold, who was a good guy, very precise, well ordered, and controlled in everything he did. And the poor man was presiding over chaos! But it all worked. The hard part for me was the schedule. Seven days on day shift, two days off. Seven days on second shift, three days off. Seven days on third shift, four days off. My body wouldn't adjust; I couldn't sleep. But, just as I'd told Marleen, I was learning a lot.

Meanwhile, I tried to keep up the house, but because it was so poorly constructed, it was not worth investing in further improvements. In the summer, we put it up for sale after making a down payment on a nice half-acre lot and a factory-built Wausau Home. The house sold quickly, and we had to rent a duplex to live in until our new home was ready. Then things started happening very fast.

In the fall, Robin started kindergarten. Then came the glitches with the new house. Our financing for the house fell through. I had made our buying decisions based on a verbal commitment, but when the steely-eyed loan committee met, they determined the house value to be less than what we needed to borrow. I spent a frantic day going to every bank in town with our package. Nobody would touch it. So we cut the package to bare bones and committed to doing much of the finish work ourselves to get to a number our original lender could live with. Then, while working on grading around the new foundation, I came down with appendicitis and lost two weeks of work.

Our new house had three bedrooms, living room, dining room, big kitchen, one and a half baths, a two car attached garage, and a full basement. The house was completed and declared ready for occupancy in February 1974. Moving day was set for Saturday during my normal four days off after completing the third shift. Thursday morning, as my shift was ending, it began to snow, heavy and wet snow. Before it was over Thursday night, we had a record snowfall accompanied by strong winds, which resulted in wide-spread power outages. Our duplex was cold and dark. Our reliable little Volkswagen was parked seven miles away in the garage of the new house. My 1967 Ford pickup was buried in snow outside the duplex. I spent the better part of Friday morning digging it out. I told Marleen that I had to go check on the new house to make sure the power was on and that nothing was frozen. The drive took almost an hour. The road, Rodney Lane, was not plowed, and there was a huge, impassable drift in front of the driveway to the new house. Leaving the Ford in the road, I rushed into the house hoping that everything would be alright. It was. The heat was on; the refrigerator was purring away. Even the phone worked! I called Marleen and told her to pack up our

Moving Up

food and some blankets and pillows and that I'd be back there as soon as possible. Then I trudged back down Rodney Lane to where my brother-in-law Dave and wife Darleen lived. I had stored my garden tractor snow blower with them and retrieved it now to clear a path to the new house. I cleared the drift in the road, cleared the driveway, and swapped the Ford for the VW.

The ride back to town was faster, and I quickly loaded the family and stuff in the car and headed back. The kids were in awe—a new house! We let them choose their rooms. There was no carpet. The walls were primed but not yet painted. The woodwork was unfinished. But it was our new house, and we spent our first night in it sleeping peacefully on the bare, painted floor.

The next morning, I called my friends, the ones that had offered to help us move. They were astonished. "What, you're still moving? Today?" Oh yeah, we were moving today! I drove to town to get the rental truck and met our friends at the duplex, which was still cold and dark. We loaded up and headed out. As we approached Rodney Lane, the town snow plow was just going through. Our second night in the new house, we slept comfortably in our own beds.

We painted and stained and varnished. Marleen did most of it while I was at work; she was better at it anyway. In the spring,

I bought eighty pounds of grass seed, tied the kids' wagon to the back of the garden tractor, sat Robin in the wagon with a handheld spreader and the sack of seeds, and drove around the yard as Robin cranked the handle on the spreader. Slowly, over time, everything got finished. Marleen's dad contributed some trees. A vegetable garden was dug. Although it was just a fifteen minute drive to work, we felt like we were in the country. We could hear the cows on the nearby farms and the trains running at night. The Franksville church was close by, a pretty old white painted sanctuary that reminded me a little of the old First Reformed Church back home. Except that, by now, Marleen and I had ceased to call Iowa or New York "home." This was home now.

I needed a change at work. The job was still interesting, but the shift changes were getting to me. I started looking around at other jobs outside the company. One day in late 1974, the personnel manager summoned me to his office on the fourth floor. Generally, you didn't want to be summoned to the fourth floor; it was best to avoid it. After I was seated, the manager, Paul Dusterhoft, said the safety and training department was exploring the idea of creating a formal training program for service fitters. Would I be interested in the job? I said sure. More tests ensued, of course, but eventually I was offered the job of training specialist and joined the management payroll as a salaried employee. My task was to evaluate the current level of training, all of which was presently done on the job, and develop a basic training curriculum for new hires. And since, once again, nobody had ever done this before, I got to do whatever I wanted.

I began by spending time in the field with most of the fifty or so service fitters in our five districts. I observed their work, the widely different practices and policies they worked under, the tools they used, and the vehicles they drove. I met with all five supervisors and their managers to discuss their views on what was important to the job.

Most of the men in the field were much older that I was, and my five years as a serviceman did not impress guys who had twenty years on the job. I wrote a report of my findings, along with some recommendations. In it, I pointed out the wide disparities in practice, equipment and technical expertise that I had observed. The report was met with horror. "You can't write stuff like this!" But that's what they'd asked me to do. Only I had to be nicer, soften it up a little, understand the politics. Okay, fine.

There was a small budget for the program, and with it I built a crude training area with working appliances. I wrote the curriculum and started training new servicemen, one on one. But I was being isolated from the rest of the safety and training department. They saw me as a disruption in their long-established routines, and the boss' need to control every detail of his kingdom didn't help when I was trying to innovate.

I was taking an evening course in real estate and earned my license. The day came at work when I'd had my fill of micromanagement, and I walked out. I called the boss from home and said I was taking a week of vacation, then packed up the family and took a trip to Nashville. When we returned, I gave my notice. Two weeks later, I quit, leaving behind a good salary and great benefits. I was also just six months shy of being vested in the company's pension plan. On April 1, 1977, I started work as a full time real estate salesman with Orth Real Estate. Never has April Fool's day been more appropriately observed.

My goal in real estate was to earn enough in my first month to equal or exceed my former salary at Wisconsin Natural Gas Company. I met that goal. I soon became the second highest producer in our office. The hours were brutal though. I'd drop everything at home to go show a house or walk around an offer to purchase. Anything to be successful.

"But you are a chosen race, a royal priesthood,
a holy nation, a people for his own possession,
that you may proclaim the excellencies of
him who called you out of darkness
into his marvelous light."
1 Peter 2:9 ESV

Chapter 16

FRIENDS AND FAMILY

Tom and Sue Stickland had remained friends, although we didn't socialize as much anymore. Tom had come to work at the gas company and had worked his way up to serviceman. They had two boys. One day they came to visit. There on the living room floor, their kids played with our kids, and I couldn't help but wonder at it. We'd never imagined that the two guys who had stumbled across frozen fields in France would one day be laughing with our children in a sunlit home in Wisconsin. One day in 1976, Sue called me early on Sunday morning to say that Tom had died. He was killed instantly when the motorcycle he was driving hit a car head on at highway speed. I'd lost a good friend.

In 1977, we bought a small used travel trailer and went camping with our friends from Gilson Street, Jim and Charley Rasmussen, at a beautiful nearby campground. It was heavily wooded with several small ponds and widely separated campsites. The owners enforced a no alcohol, low noise policy that made it a pleasure to be there with our children. Jim and Charley had two children, a boy and a girl, and as we camped side by side, the children played, and we enjoyed the respite from the city and our work.

On Sunday, Charley invited us to go to church with them back in town. Christ Church, a United Methodist congregation, was large, about twelve hundred members. There were two Sunday worship services, two Sunday School sessions, three choirs (adult, youth and children's), two youth groups, and a mission program. Right then, I wanted our daughters to have the chance to participate in all of that. Soon afterward, we moved our membership to that congregation. God was about to do great work in me and my family over the next two decades.

But first, I became a Girl Scout Dad.

When Robin was eight years old in 1976, Marleen went to the first Brownie meeting of the year to get Robin signed up. Naturally, Marleen was asked to be a parent helper. Over the next several meetings, however, she was asked to do more and more until she became Robin's Brownie troop leader, working with another mom who was her assistant. The troop started meeting in our basement. Then the assistant leader quit. That's when I joined the Girl Scouts of America as a Girl Scout Dad (it's an official title, you can look it up) and became my wife's assistant leader. She was terrific at it. Using the Girl Scout manual and her own creativity, the meetings were great fun with crafts and learning and songs. I'd play the guitar, and the girls would sing along. One of our favorites was "Goober Peas," a silly civil war song made popular by the Kingston Trio.

Some of the girls were with us for six years or more, graduating from the light brown Brownie outfit to the grown up green of the Girl Scouts. They were a very diverse group, and we enjoyed watching them mature, forming strong friendships and building good character.

Starr entered the whole adventure when she was eight, and then we had two troops. She was way ahead of the curve, having been around the older girls for so many years. We'd put on skits and invite the parent to come. One Christmas, I wrote a play telling the story of Jesus' birth from Mary's donkey's point of view. Another time, the older girls created a haunted house maze in our basement using sheets hung from the ceiling. It was so effective that a couple of the Brownies ran away crying in fear. But after some cookies and milk, all was well again.

We went camping at some of the beautiful Girl Scout campgrounds in Racine and nearby. I was the designated fire builder (really!). We bought an eleven-passenger van to haul the troop around.

One epic weekend, we took all the Brownies and a few of the older girls to Camp Singing Hills for a weekend. We arrived Friday evening and settled into the platform tents at our campsite, which was heavily wooded and located at the base of a steep hill. The outdoor toilets were located at the end of a narrow path up the hill. Marleen prepared campfire stew, and it was delicious. After supper, Starr became ill with a fever. Robin had gone up the hill to the toilets when suddenly the sky grew very dark. There was a sound like an oncoming train as the wind picked up. Robin came racing down the hill yelling "tornado!" How she didn't fall and break her neck I'll never know. I began to pray very hard and very fast, "God, you've given us responsibility for all these little girls. Please show me what to do and protect us." We quickly gathered the girls and took them to a nearby building, sort of a lodge. We managed to get in, and I wanted to try for the basement. But it was too small. So we spent the night on the floor, huddled in blankets, listening to the howling wind and pouring rain.

In the morning, it was still drizzling. The girls were damp and sleepy, so I suggested we pack it in and go home. But Marleen was determined that the girls be fed first. She set up the "buddy burners" (inverted coffee cans with wax-filled burners underneath) and proceeded to make pancakes and sausage on these primitive stoves until everyone was fed. Then we packed up the wet gear and the damp girls and went home. Starr had scarlet fever.

I'll never forget those precious years. Marleen did such a great job with the girls, giving them a chance to grow in exciting new ways. Years later, we watched proudly as some of the girls graduated high school with honors and high achievement. Decades later, I found one of the girls on Facebook. She'd just "friended" Robin. I suggested a reunion of the group, and she said she'd come if I promised to play my guitar and sing "Goober Peas" one more time.

Meanwhile, I was trying to make a living. Sometimes, the real estate job was very satisfying. Getting to know a family that was in the market for a new home, finding the right house, leading them through the process, helping to obtain financing were all part of the service designed to put buyers and sellers together. And it was a booming market just then. But it was a merry-go-round moving ever faster. The firm made me vice president (mostly to keep me from leaving) and tasked me to oversee and train the sales staff, still expecting me to keep up my own high listing and sales performance. The salary was nice, but it was really a draw against future commissions. I was drinking more and spending too much time away from my family. And there were temptations to stray everywhere. I realized I had a choice to make: keep my career or keep my family. My vows to make family number one made for an easy decision. Not so easy was, now what do I do? I printed and mailed out about a hundred blind resumes with a standard cover letter saying, in effect, "What have you got? I'm the guy who can do it!"

Miraculously, I actually got a job with that tactic. The A. O. Smith Corporation wanted to get more energy efficient and had created a new job awkwardly titled "combustion supervisor." No, my job was not to burn the place down (although I *did* have some experience in that area) but to examine the gas-fired processing equipment and recommend changes to save gas. I worked with an outside consultant who taught me a lot about industrial processes and energy efficiency. I wrote procedures and developed training to implement them. In that, I got involved with the company's excellent video department where I learned how to write scripts and use graphics to teach employees about combustion. The manufacturing plant was at once fascinating and depressing. The big machines banged out parts, and the huge ovens heat treated the parts. It was loud and fast and amazing. The enmity between management and the multiple unions made for a hostile, tension filled environment. And I was caught in the middle, a tie-wearing "suit" whose job it was to help the union guys learn to do their jobs better. It was not where I wanted to be.

So I prayed. I asked God, quite boldly and specifically, for a new job, one that would be close to home, with a forty-hour work week, with predictable hours so I could serve my church and adequate income to support my family. Shortly thereafter, I was served with a permanent layoff notice and given two week's severance pay.

I went home to tell Marleen. I explained that with the two week's severance check and the proceeds from my employee stock plan, we had enough money for about six weeks. I assured her that everything would work out, that God had a plan.

A year before, in 1979, there had been another event that reinforced the faith I had in God to work wonders. Marleen and the girls went on a weekend camp without me. I sat at home, beating myself up about my job, my life, and my drinking. The drinking had to stop. I sat on the edge of our bed and began to pray, pleading with God to help me get alcohol out of my life. I heard no voices, saw no visions, nor did angels sing. Instead, confident in God's power to save, I got up and poured the gin, the bourbon, the wine, and the beer down the drain in the kitchen and threw the bottles and cans into the trash. When Marleen returned home with our daughters, I told her I was done drinking. The alcohol was gone, and no more would come into our house. That's the way it has remained until this very day. Thanks be to God!

Out of work now in the summer of 1980, I searched the want ads, networked with friends, and kept up my hopes. As the six weeks were winding down and the cash was dwindling, I saw an ad in the local paper: "Gas Control Specialist. Apply at Wisconsin Natural Gas Company." With hat in hand, I humbly walked into the personnel office and asked for the job. After determining that I'd not burned any bridges with upper management, they hired me back. It was unprecedented. This company valued employee

Friends and Family

loyalty like a family, and rehiring people who had quit just didn't happen.

Not only did I get rehired, but because of a fairly new company policy, my pension, vacation time, and other benefits were credited with my previous nine and a half years of service. Everything was restored as if I had never left. So two parts of my prayer were answered. Six weeks after my layoff, I returned to work at the gas company.

The dreaded rotating schedule began again, but I was determined to stick it out and trusted God for a good outcome. About seven weeks after I was back, Paul Dusterhoft again summoned me to his fourth floor office. "Would you be interested in a management job?" he asked. "That's why I came back," I said. He told me that a new position was being created, and he thought I might fit the bill. Again, testing was done (I often felt like a lab rat).

Two weeks later, I was out in the garage changing oil on the van when the phone rang. Wiping the oil off my hands, I grabbed the phone. Joe Honeck, the customer services manager, was calling me to offer me the job of superintendent—residential conservation at a monthly salary of $2,125. My hands were shaking. "If you want to think about it and talk it over with your wife, you can call me on Monday and give me your decision," he said. "I'll take it," I said.

About four months after I'd prayed my prayer for stability, I had a new job close to home, regular hours, adequate salary, and outstanding benefits. God is awesome indeed. But He was still not through with me.

"For I am not ashamed of the gospel, for it is
the power of God for salvation to
everyone who believes..."
Romans 1:16 ESV

Chapter 17

NOT QUITE BILLY GRAHAM

In 1982, our pastor suggested I attend an upcoming lay speaker class. The program was designed to train lay people for preaching and leadership in the church, including filling in for vacationing pastors. I enrolled in the six-week class, earned my certificate, and received the endorsement of our church council. On Sunday, April 18, 1982, I preached my first sermon as a guest speaker at Trinity United Methodist Church in Racine. What a joy it was to serve God by preaching His word. At the time of this writing in 2016, I have preached over 163 sermons. Not nearly half as many as Billy

Graham preached in a good year, but still many more than I ever thought was possible.

I started a men's Bible study on Wednesday evenings for guys who were waiting while their kids were in choir practice. As our daughters grew older and got involved in the youth group, I became a volunteer helper to our youth pastor. For five years, I helped lead teen work groups participating in the Appalachia Service Project, a home repair ministry. I helped lead youth retreats, wrote scripts for our weekends, and wrote an Easter liturgy for our youth-led sunrise service.

I was elected lay leader in our congregation and, as such, participated in all the committees and boards with the goal of keeping our eyes and hearts focused on heavenly things. Then, I was chosen to be lay member to the Annual Conference of the United Methodist Church in Wisconsin. Led by the bishop, I, along with lay people and pastors from every congregation, participated in the multi-day event, listening to and approving reports, voting on budgets and petitions, and participating in the ordination of new pastors.

At the conclusion of the ordination rites, the entire assembly would participate in Holy Communion, with the newly-ordained pastors serving loaf and cup at stations around the auditorium. There were usually about sixteen hundred people in attendance, so it was a lengthy process. I would seek out the station where someone I knew was serving, then go stand in the back of the auditorium to observe and pray. Often I'd cry, partly in joy over the sacredness of the moment and partly in sorrow that I was not one of those who had just been ordained.

Many times I started to explore what it would take to become ordained, and each time two obstacles kept me from moving forward. The first was my lack of a college degree. Four years of college and three years of seminary were out of the question with a family to support. The second was doubt about my call. Preaching was what I wanted to do; pastoring a congregation was another thing entirely. Every time I preached, someone would inevitably say, "You missed your calling" or "Why aren't you a pastor?" Although my heart often yearned for a full-time ministry of preaching the Word of God, my response to these statements was that in being a Christian husband, father, and businessman, I was doing exactly what God wanted me to do. I hope that on judgment day I will hear, "Well done!" and not "Why did you not...?" My salvation is certain because of what Christ has already done on the cross, and I have to trust that my Sovereign God has led me on exactly His chosen path.

Aimless Life, Awesome God

The Annual Conferences I attended, and there were many, were times of blessing and times of trouble. The battle between so-called human reason and Biblical truth was on full display. There were pastors and bishops whose faith was in their own reason, who believed social action, diversity, and tolerance to be the true marks of a Christian, while they ignored the gospel truth that we are all sinners in need of a Savior. What they did not tolerate was belief in the infallible truth of the Bible, especially the idea of substitutionary atonement of Christ on the cross. In all my years of teaching, preaching, and leading in the United Methodist Church, I sensed that people were hungry for the truth, but were being fed humanistic lies by the hierarchy of the church.

Each time I was called to fill the pulpit at some church in town or in our own congregation, I would first pray for the people. After reading the lectionary scriptures for that week, I'd pray to find what God wanted me to preach, then craft the sermon. In the early years, I just used notes, trusting the Holy Spirit and my memory to provide the words. Gradually I began writing it out, still leaving room for the spontaneous word that might come and help make the point. I also determined that every message had to contain a gospel message aimed at the one person in the room who had not yet come to faith. There were no "alter calls," but the gospel call would always be in the message.

Both the United Methodist Church and the Reformed Church in America offer a pathway for people like me, something called a licensed pastor. Someone with the gifts and call could be assigned to serve a congregation while undergoing a course of study under the authority of the denomination. This would eliminate the college and seminary requirements, and help the denominations fill vacant pulpits. As intriguing as these programs were, going forward meant uprooting my family and asking them to sacrifice for my dream. I couldn't do it.

In 1991, I was surprised and delighted when I learned that my boyhood friend Bob Zittel had left his career and enrolled in seminary at the age of forty-six. He was ordained as a pastor in 1994. In 1995, I drove out to upstate New York to spend a weekend with Bob and Barbara. He was serving two congregations: one big, one small. On Sunday, Bob invited me to assist him in worship at the smaller church. We prayed together before the service, and I had tears in my eyes for the joy of seeing my good friend leading his flock. I read the scripture, we sang together, and Bob preached. It was delightful.

It turned out that Bob and I had another connection; we had each participated in a

"Walk to Emmaus" men's retreat in 1990 almost simultaneously, he in New York and I in Wisconsin. The weekend was modeled after the Roman Catholic "Cusillo" movement, which was created to train laymen and prepare them for leadership in the church. It was Bob's involvement in the "Walk" that led to his entering the ministry.

The weekend consists of fifteen talks, mostly presented by laymen. The attendees, or pilgrims, are divided up into table groups that remain together for the entire time. Each table has a leader and assistant leader. After each talk, discussion ensues, and a poster is made depicting the results of the discussion. There is much singing, eating, and fellowship. Each day begins with worship, and Holy Communion is celebrated as well. It was a warm and inspiring experience.

After the weekend, we were urged to join a reunion group for weekly fellowship and accountability. The group I joined met every Wednesday at 6:30 AM at a local restaurant. Following a carefully scripted outline, we'd pray, read scripture, and share how we were growing in witness and service. I attended that group for twenty years.

The following year, I was asked to give one of the talks. In subsequent years I served as assistant table leader, table leader, song leader, assistant director, and lay director, each time giving one of the talks. I grew a little every time I served on a team, seven times in all. I watched as other men's lives were changed by the growth in faith they experienced during their "Walk."

God was using me in my own congregation in the wider church and in small groups to spread His word and serve His people in ways I had never imagined I could.

"And my God will supply every need of
yours according to his riches
in glory in Christ Jesus."
Philippians 4:19 ESV

Chapter 18

AN ORDINARY WITNESS

All the while, God was helping me live out my faith in my work, blessing me with opportunity and success and giving me strength in times of hardship.

As Superintendent—Residential Conservation—I hated that title, it took up most of a business card and nobody knew what it meant—I was responsible for the development and implementation of government mandated energy conservation programs, in particular, the federally-mandated Residential Conservation Service program. The Public Service Commission (PSC) of Wisconsin made the rules and monitored the results. The main component of this drive to save energy was a very detailed, computer-generated home energy audit.

Our job was to convince our customers to have these free energy audits, then assist them with the implementation of our recommendations. This meant the company had to hire about fifty energy auditors, and I had to hire staff to train them and oversee the programs. My job was simple, really. Convince our customers to use less of our product (which made me an unpopular guy on the fourth floor), inflict the costs of these programs on all our customers through our rates (another lose-lose situation), and keep the Public Service Commission happy so we could run our business (sort of a win if I succeeded). I determined that we would do the very best job possible to serve and please our customers and make the PSC very satisfied with our efforts.

Hiring staff for my team created a unique opportunity. Utility companies were populated by engineers and accountants, especially among the management. This was necessitated by the nature of the business; safety and reliability are paramount, and regulatory scrutiny is justifiably intense. Since accounting and engineering were male-dominated professions, men ran the show. Women were mostly clerks and secretaries. But as the customer service side of the business grew, so did the opportunities increase for well-educated, skilled women.

My department grew quickly from four people, two of whom were clerks, to ten in a short period of time. Different skill sets were called for and so three of the program managers I hired were women. Terry Orlick, Ellen Schneider, and Barbara Bras became a fantastic team. In order for us to succeed, I knew that it was my job to help each one of them to achieve their highest potential. They were smart and energetic, so I just let them run with their ideas, counseling and mentoring when necessary. The big battle was behind the scenes. I gave these women every credit they were due. I fought against every negative stereotype during annual performance reviews, where I had to convince management and human resource raters that these women were making a great contribution and were worthy of the same pay raises that the more favored occupations were getting. I didn't always win. In fact, I got so angry during one session that I had to leave the office afterwards and go home to cool off. Gradually, the true worth of these three became more and more accepted. Eventually, each one of them moved on to higher and better positions than mine both inside and outside the company. Their growth and achievement was the most satisfying experience in all my

An Ordinary Witness

years as a manager, and I'm more proud of them than any other accomplishment in my career.

Although it was tedious to be under the thumb of the PSC, I was able to achieve the two goals of customer satisfaction and regulatory blessing. We had a great team of energy auditors in the field that provided top-notch advice and assistance to our customers. We met or exceeded every numerical goal in terms of audits performed and energy saved. As I grew into the job, I assumed leadership roles at the state and regional level. I chaired the statewide Auditor Training Committee, the Inter-Utility Committee, and the Mid-America Residential Gas Council. Each of these positions brought more opportunities to lead and to speak before large groups. I testified at PSC rate hearings, making the case for our successful programs while trying to minimize the costs of regulatory compliance.

My opportunities for Christian witness were many. As a non-drinker, I became a favorite and welcome designated driver at the numerous cocktail hours, banquets, and business dinners that were part of the job. That I used vacation time to go on the mission trips with the youth of our church was well known. I found other Christians in the company and among my outside contacts, and we'd share our faith. I did my very best to treat all people well, and often had the chance to explain that I was the way I was because of Christ. Except for my occasional outbursts of anger, I did my best to live out my faith, and people noticed.

In 1993, the company was engaged in a massive restructuring effort. I was part of one planning group, exploring new methods, new divisions of responsibility, new positions, and new organizational structure. It was exciting to be part of the discussion, and my hope was that we'd be a better, more responsive company than ever. My other hope was that I could get out of the conservation business and move on to something new. We were all eager to see the new organization take shape.

In early January 1994, just before my fifty-first birthday, I was summoned to the vice president's office on the fourth floor. "Here we go!" I thought. "Where will I be on the organizational chart?" Stu Erbe, the VP, had me sit down and told me two things were about to happen. "The first is dramatic," he said, "the second is traumatic." I wonder how long he'd practiced those exact words. The first event was that we had just merged with a small gas utility located to our south and that one year hence we would be merging with our parent company, Wisconsin Electric Power Company and become a combined gas and electric utility.

An Ordinary Witness

Okay, I thought, that's exciting. Second, he said, "When the new organization chart comes out at the end of the month, your name will not be on it." My options, he explained, were to find another position at Wisconsin Electric where, according to him, "you don't have many friends" or leave the company and find another job. I had until the end of February.

"Don't tell anyone about this," he said.

"I have to tell my people," I said. I shook his hand and said I understood how hard this must have been for him.

I gathered my staff in my office and told them what was going to happen. They were shocked; someone cried. I told them that they had to do what was best for themselves, to decide whether to stay or to go. I said I didn't know if any of them would be affected directly, but that everything was going to change. I urged each one to continue to give their work their very best effort for the sake of their own dignity and self-worth. Later, I went home, told Marleen, and felt as if I was going to die.

I said to myself, "I'm fifty-one years old with no college degree, years of experience that no longer apply in a rapidly changing industry, and a daughter still in college. Where will I find a job?"

But then I took my own advice. The devotional I was using at the time, *A Guide to*

Prayer for All God's People had this prayer that I read the very next morning:

> "O God, sovereign Lord over all creation, without whom all purposes are futile, grant me today the assistance of your Spirit. In all the surprises and changes of life, may I fix my heart upon you, so that your eternal purposes may be fixed in me. In the name of Jesus, who came to make your eternal purpose clear. Amen."

I made copies to take to work. As colleagues began to get their notices, I shared my prayer with them. I took Marleen out to dinner and assured her that everything would work out, that we'd be okay. I worked hard at my job, updated my resume, and started networking with people I knew in the utility industry. The deadline for my decision, stay or go, was February 28.

I was scheduled to attend a training session in Minneapolis for a few days in January. There was a new vice president on the fourth floor, Chuck Govin, a man I'd served with on a few committees in the past. I went to his office and said I was going away for a few days, and I did not want to return to find my desk cleaned out. Then I said, "When I get back, I'll sign the papers and get on with the rest of my life." He said, "Don't sign anything! I have something I want you to do." Filled with hope, I went home, dropped my keys on the dresser, and cried my eyes out. When Marleen came to see what the matter was, I sobbed, "Somebody needs me. They still need me!"

"I will instruct you and teach you in the way
you should go; I will counsel you
with my eye upon you."
Psalm 32:8 ESV

Chapter 19

TO BOLDLY GO

The task I was given was this. Although the company was growing within its franchise territory, it had never been interested in looking outside its borders. My job was to do that, to analyze the whole state of Wisconsin, locate areas ripe for expansion of natural gas service, and make proposals to acquire the territory. Like so many of my previous jobs, this one had never been done before in our company. I was to be a one-man operation, coordinating with engineers, accountants, and regulatory staff to put together complete proposals. I got to pick my own title, "Manager—Territory Development," pick my own boss, Chuck

Govin, keep my old office, keep my current salary and benefits, and chart my own course, without any staff. Things like that just don't happen!

In the ensuing months, most of the officers and mangers above me were eased out, including Stu Erbe, who had given me the bad news. Many of my friends were also forced out.

I had no idea how to do what they wanted me to do until I received a forwarded email about the potential invasion of a Michigan gas utility into our electric service territory on the Wisconsin-Michigan border. So began the most enjoyable and productive years of my career. Armed with maps and a notebook, I spent half my time driving around the state, counting houses and businesses and estimating distances to the nearest gas pipeline. Back at the office, I'd put together crazy proposals no one had ever considered before and persuaded management to just do it. I had a big map of the state of Wisconsin in the office which was divided up into townships and color-coded with the franchise territories of all the gas utilities in the state. There was more white space than colored space on the map, and it was my job to color in lots of new towns with the Wisconsin Natural Gas color.

Every project was a battle, getting the accountants to analyze and buy in, getting the engineers to see how it could be built, and convincing the PSC to let us go ahead. I'd meet with town boards to get their approval and with local civic groups and business leaders to gain their support. Using crude maps and a few facts and figures, I'd explain how the whole community would benefit if natural gas service were to be made available. At the later stages of a project, I'd appear at PSC-conducted public hearings to make our case. It was a wild and hugely satisfying adventure, the polar opposite of the regulatory-driven conservation stuff I'd done for the past thirteen years.

The craziest project was our expansion into Vilas County, on the Wisconsin-Michigan border. It was the largest expansion ever in our company's history, involving all or parts of ten townships. It took three years from proposal to approval and another year for the preliminary construction. We connected thousands of new customers.

When I first got this reprieve from termination, I'd set a goal for myself: that I would be able to hang on with the company until I reached the age of fifty-five, which was the earliest I could retire with health benefits. I made it to age fifty-eight.

Since I received the first layoff notice in 1994, I'd survived two more mergers and a major reorganization precipitated by yet another pending merger that ultimately failed. But the fourth merger ended my career. At the time of the merger with Wisconsin Gas Company, the state's largest gas utility, I was actually doing two jobs, territory expansion and gas marketing. I had a small staff and we were responsible for the marketing effort required to get customers to sign up in the new territories we'd acquired. But as the bigger company swallowed our smaller one, some people had to go.

My name was on a short list of people who, due to their age and years of service, would be eligible for two programs: an enhanced severance package and an advanced retirement package. I took both.

I retired February 1, 2001 after a little over thirty years with the company. At my retirement party, I tried to remember and thank all the people who'd helped me be successful in my career. It was impossible; the list was too long. I said that nothing I had accomplished would have been possible without the help of others, mentors, peers and staff. My manager, Bob Whitefoot, opened his remarks by saying, "One thing I know about Bob Frohlich is that he always knew how to balance his faith, his family, and his career."

Our two daughters were there and gave me the gift of a test flight at a local airport, fulfilling a dream of mine to fly a plane at least once. I thanked Marleen for being a great wife. In closing, I picked up my guitar and sang this song by an unknown author:

"In His time, in His time,
He makes all things beautiful in His time.
Lord please show me every day
As you're teaching me Your way
That you do just what you say, in Your time."

"In Your time, in Your time,
You make all things beautiful, in Your time.
Lord my life to You I bring,
May each song I have to sing,
Be to You a lovely thing
In Your time."

So maybe that's why I never became the next Billy Graham. And God is still not done with me.

"The righteous flourish like the palm tree and grow like a cedar in Lebanon. They are planted in the house of the Lord; they flourish in the courts of our God. They still bear fruit in old age; they are ever full of sap and green, to declare that the Lord is upright; he is my rock, and there is no unrighteousness in him.:
Psalm 92:12–15 ESV

Chapter 20

WHATEVER HAPPENED TO...?

My life story began with my family, and I want to close the book on their stories.

My grandparents, the Burtners, moved to Florida in 1975 to be close to their daughter. William Burtner died in 1977 and Elsbeth died in 1984.

In their will, my grandparents left two thirds of their house to my mom, Ursula, and one third to me. I immediately signed over my portion to Mom, telling her that I wanted her, finally, to have something all her own. Ed Bonn had left her sometime before this and moved to northern Florida where he died in 1989. Mom sold the house and moved into a trailer. After being diagnosed with cancer and refusing treatment, she moved to San Antonio, Texas to live with my sister Helen. Mom died in June 1992, while I was on my way out to see her. I conducted her funeral service with just my sisters, Helen and Joanne, and Joanne's son, Jeremy, in attendance. Mom was penniless when she died.

In 1993, I was summoned to Florida by my sister Joanne and her husband Jack. My dad, Bill Frohlich, was living with them, and they needed the space for Jack's son, Matthew. We found a small, comfortable, furnished condominium which I bought for him. It was not far from Joanne's house, and she watched over him until he died suddenly in 2010. I donated his Boy Scout awards and memorabilia to the Poppenhusen museum in College Point so that his contribution to scouting would always be remembered.

Robert William Kaufman died in Oklahoma in 1998. In 2010, I was contacted by a long-lost cousin from College Point, Judy Fluker, Robert Kaufman's niece. Through her, I learned more about my father and the ghost family I had in New York. I found I'd had an aunt, uncle, and

Whatever happened to...?

two cousins, Judy and Susan. They, like me, had never learned exactly what happened back in the 1940s.

My brother John's marriage did not last very long. Although he was very intelligent and had enjoyed much success working in the food service industry in Canada, something happened that troubled him and changed him. He came to me in 1991, broke, and stayed with us for a while. I sent him to Florida, where he reunited with Joanne and mom and found work.

In 1998, John called me from Florida to say he'd lost everything in a tornado and that he wanted to come stay with me again. I flew him up to Racine, bought him clothes and a car, and got him a job. Eventually he settled in Green Bay, Wisconsin, found steady work, made some friends, and enjoyed his life. But there was always something of a dark cloud about him. We'd talk on the phone, and I'd correspond with him, often sharing the gospel. He rejected the faith, favoring his own reason instead. Each year, on John's birthday, I'd go visit, and we'd play golf and enjoy a meal together.

In 2014, John developed lung cancer. While he was being treated, I went to visit him in his shabby little room in an old converted strip motel. He was very weak, and his breathing was troubled. We talked for a while, and then I took him to lunch, which he enjoyed immensely. Afterward, I asked if I could pray with him, and he consented. Two months later, in early February, a doctor called me from Green Bay. John was dying and refusing further treatment. The next morning, I drove up to see him. He was thin, haggard, and sweating, wearing an oxygen mask. He asked for the mask to be removed so we could talk. I agreed with him that further treatment would not restore him to health but only prolong his suffering. They gave John a sedative. I read Psalm 103 to him and prayed with him. When it was time for me to leave, I told him that I loved him, that his family loved him, and that God loved him. I kissed him and went home. A few days later, John died peacefully in the hospital.

I arranged for John's body to be cremated, then bought a cemetery plot near our home. My pastor and a few of my friends held a graveside service. John's grave marker reads, "My brother; my friend."

My sisters still live in Florida.

In all these things, God gave me the privilege of serving my family. Though we were troubled and not always close, I loved them.

Both our daughters, Robin and Starr, graduated from college, the first in our family to do so. Robin earned a degree in education, got married, and, with her husband Tim, is raising three children. Starr earned a business degree in accounting and went to work in that field two days after graduation. She has had a very successful career in the financial services field. Marleen and I are so proud of both our daughters, well pleased with the fine women they have become.

Marleen and I have been married for fifty years now. There have been many joys and many trials in our life together. The amazing grace of God has blessed us in the joys and sustained us in the trials.

As I look back at the aimless, wandering path of my youth, at my rebellion, my anger, my running away, I can't help but marvel at the outcome. I wrote this book to praise my awesome God for His grace and mercy in saving me through the blood of Jesus my Savior. I praise and thank Him for putting people and opportunities in my path. This life—this incredibly wonderful life I have lived—has been more than I ever could have imagined. Every morning when I pray, my final request to God is "Bless me to be a blessing." I pray that this story will be just that.

"Remember not the sins of my youth or my transgressions; according to your steadfast love remember me, for the sake of your goodness, O Lord!" Psalm 25:7 ESV

Soli Deo Gloria!